In *The Word In Life Study Bible*, Y[...] Paul's Letters Like They Were Written to You.

The Super–Powerful Gospel

The salvation described in Paul's letter to the Romans extends to all aspects of life, all times and places, and all kinds of people. See the Introduction to Romans.

Nobody's Perfect

God has reached out to humanity despite its imperfect ways. See Romans 3:9–18.

Is Work a Curse?

The Bible calls work and its fruit a gift from God. See Romans 8:20.

The Liberation of Creation

As God's people, we affirm both the salvation of persons and the transformation of places. See Romans 8:21–22.

Do You Suffer from "Comparisonitis"?

What needs to change in your self–assessment for you to see yourself as God sees you? See Romans 12:3.

Matters of Conscience

Plenty of issues have managed to divide believers today. Does Paul offer any perspective on settling such disputes? See Romans 14:1–23.

Workplace Myths

Distorted views of work have taken on mythical proportions
in Western culture. See 1 Corinthians 3:9.

The Ultimate Performance Review

When the smoke clears, what will be left of your life?
See 1 Corinthians 3:13–15.

Practical Lessons on Marriage

Marriage was undergoing profound changes in Paul's time just as it is today.
See 1 Corinthians 7:1.

Women and Work in the Ancient World

The New Testament shows that women carried out a wide range of tasks.
See 1 Corinthians 7:32–35.

The New Covenant

God has made a new agreement with humanity, based on the death
and resurrection of Jesus Christ. See 1 Corinthians 11:25.

Enemies Become Family and Friends

God makes believers into a new family—we are now brothers and sisters
in Christ. See 1 Corinthians 16:9–20.

Accountability

As believers, we are accountable not only for our actions, but also for our attitudes. See 2 Corinthians 2:5–11.

The Judgment Seat

Are you paying attention to your "deeds done in the body"? See 2 Corinthians 5:10.

Welcome to Stressful Living

The stress of obeying Christ is preparing us for riches we will enjoy for eternity. See 2 Corinthians 6:3–10.

Integrity in the Face of Competition

When you face a competitive situation, are you tempted to do whatever it takes to win? See 2 Corinthians 10:1.

Spiritual Authority

Do you exercise leadership in order to accomplish the best interests of those who follow you? See 2 Corinthians 13:10.

Discover the Truths of God's Word for You and Your World.

Romans, 1 & 2 Corinthians

The Word IN LIFE™ Study Bible

THOMAS NELSON PUBLISHERS
Nashville • Atlanta • London • Vancouver

ACKNOWLEDGMENTS

Romans 8:20: "Is Work a Curse?" Adapted by permission from Doug Sherman and William Hendricks, *Your Work Matters to God,* NavPress, 1987.

Romans 14:5: quotation from Elton Trueblood, *Your Other Vocation,* Harper & Brothers, 1952, used by permission of HarperCollins Publishers.

1 Corinthians 1:26: "Ten Myths About Christianity, Myth #5: Christianity Is Just a Crutch for the Weak." Adapted by permission from *Ten Myths About Christianity* by Michael Green and Gordon Carkner, Lion Publishing, 1988.

1 Corinthians 7:17: excerpt from *A Severe Mercy* by Sheldon Vanauken. Copyright ©1977, 1980 by Sheldon Vanauken. Reprinted by permission of HarperCollins Publishers Inc.

1 Corinthians 13:12: quotation from Pete Hammond, *Marketplace Networks,* InterVarsity Christian Fellowship of the USA, 1990.

1 Corinthians 15:9–10: "Ten Myths About Christianity, Myth #6: People Become Christians Through Social Conditioning." Adapted by permission from *Ten Myths About Christianity* by Michael Green and Gordon Carkner, Lion Publishing, 1988.

2 Corinthians 4:2: "A Code of Ethics for Christian Witness." Used by permission of InterVarsity Christian Fellowship of the USA.

CONTENTS

INTRODUCTION

This edition of Romans, 1 & 2 Corinthians is part of *The Word In Life Study Bible,* the beginning of a new generation of study Bibles. Its purpose is to help you discover ways to relate the Word of God to you and the world you live in. This Bible makes it easy to bring the Word into your own world by taking you right into the world of the Bible.

The Word In Life Study Bible helps you get a clear understanding of God's Word by focusing on the surroundings of the biblical narrative. Stimulating articles get you thinking about how to relate the teachings of God's Word to life. The articles raise questions about what it means to live for God in today's world—about what a believer's role in the world is—and about how the Word in one life can touch the lives of others.

Features about the people, places, and customs of Paul's world make the teachings of the Bible more vivid. You'll find friends in the Word of God. You'll feel at home where they lived. You'll discover that people aren't much different now than they were two thousand years ago. And you'll see that God's Word is more useful than you ever realized.

Explore the following pages and take a closer look at *The Word In Life Study Bible*—what it's meant to do, what it looks like, and how it works.

WHY THIS KIND OF PUBLICATION?

Someone has well said that Scripture was not written merely to be studied, but to change our lives. Likewise, James exhorts us to be "doers of the word, and not hearers only" (James 1:22). And Jesus said, "By this My Father is glorified, that you bear much fruit; so you will be my disciples" (John 15:8). Clearly, the point of God's Word is not to make us "smarter sinners" but to help us become more like Jesus Christ by making the Word of God part of our lives.

However, applying biblical truth in this day and age is far from easy. In the first place, the fact that the Bible was written thousands of years ago in a different culture can sometimes make it difficult to understand. And even if we grasp what the writers were saying to their original readers, we still must make the connection to our own situation today. In the end, many people wonder: can Scripture really make any difference in our complex, modern world? Yes it can, and this publication helps to show the way. ◆

A "USER-FRIENDLY" STUDY BIBLE

THE WORD IN LIFE STUDY BIBLE HELPS YOU UNDERSTAND THE BIBLICAL TEXT.

Before you can apply Scripture, you must understand what Scripture means. That's why The Word In Life Study Bible provides the kind of information you'll need to make sense of what the biblical text is talking about. The articles and other information (see below) provide the "who, what, when, where, how, and why" behind scores of passages, in an interesting, easy-to-understand way. Not only do they offer insight into the text, they also help you to understand the context of those passages, so that you can connect the words and events of biblical times with today.

THE WORD IN LIFE STUDY BIBLE HELPS YOU APPLY SCRIPTURE TO EVERYDAY LIFE.

"Wow! This is the kind of Bible I need in my life," one reader said. "It just makes Scripture come alive. It's contemporary. It's relevant." As you read The Word In Life Study Bible, you won't have to search and struggle for ways to apply God's Word; the articles suggest numerous possibilities for how Scripture makes a difference. That's especially helpful if you're one who is strapped for time or likes to quickly get to the point.

THE WORD IN LIFE STUDY BIBLE CHALLENGES YOU TO DEVELOP YOUR OWN THINKING.

You won't find pat answers or a "packaged" theology in this study Bible. Instead, the articles are designed to provoke your thinking by relating the text of Scripture to the issues of today, providing information to guide your thinking. Sometimes the commentary will raise a question without answering it; sometimes it will suggest possible answers. Often it will point out things that you may not have considered before. The articles don't pretend to address every issue raised by the biblical text or to solve every theological problem. But they're guaranteed to make you think!

THE WORD IN LIFE STUDY BIBLE INTRODUCES YOU TO THE PEOPLE OF SCRIPTURE.

For too many readers, the Bible can seem dull and lifeless, a book that only scholars and mystics might find interesting. But Scripture comes alive once we discover the people in the text. The Word In Life Study Bible *is* designed to help you do that, to "make friends" with some of the fascinating characters that God chose to include in His Word. Almost fifty of them receive special attention through "Personality Profiles" that summarize what we know of them (see below). Even though these people lived long ago, you'll find that you have far more in common with them than you have differences. They experienced many of the same things you do. By learning what God did in their lives, you'll gain insight into what God is doing in yours.

THE WORD IN LIFE STUDY BIBLE MAKES THE BIBLE EASY TO READ.

"I know I should read the Bible more, but to be honest, I just don't have time!" Have you ever felt that way? If so, The Word In Life Study Bible *is for you*. It was designed for busy people. In the first place, you'll enjoy how easy it is to read the New King James Version. A modern translation that preserves the stylistic beauty of the King James Version, the NKJV presents the eternal Word of God in everyday language that people can understand. You'll also find the material presented in bite-size units, with section headings to mark the text. The Scriptures are accompanied not by long, drawn out treatises, but by straight-to-the-point articles and other information presented in simple, easily grasped terms. ◆

FEATURES TO LOOK FOR

INTRODUCTORY ARTICLES

At the beginning of a book of the Bible you'll find information that explains why the book is important and what to pay attention to as you read it. You'll learn something of the background behind the book, including who the author and original readers were. You'll also get an idea of the issues the book addresses through a table of contents that describes some of the articles you'll find alongside the text.

CONSIDER THIS

(symbols enlarged)

As mentioned above, God intended His Word to change people's lives. That's why occasionally you'll find a symbol that refers you to a nearby article relating in some way to the text indicated. These articles help to explain the Scriptural passages and highlight the significance of biblical truths for modern readers. In articles with this symbol, ways are offered for you to **consider** how the passage applies to your life and the world around you.

FOR YOUR INFO

This symbol indicates articles that primarily offer **information** about the text or its cultural context. Knowing the background of a biblical passage will help you understand it more accurately and make it more useful to you.

PERSONALITY PROFILES

One of the goals that the editors of The Word In Life Study Bible *had in developing their material was to introduce readers to the* **people** *of the Scriptures, including those who lived and worked in public places. One of the important ways that this study Bible does that is through personality profiles that highlight various individuals. These are not biographies, but summaries of what the Bible tells us about the person, what can be reasonably inferred from the text, and what other sources report about his or her life and legacy.*

YOU ARE THERE

One of the most important windows on understanding the text of Scripture is knowing the **places** where the events occurred. Unfortunately, ancient localities are unknown to most modern readers. The cities of Acts, for example, are little more than dots on a map for most of us. Yet when we examine the geography of the New Testament, we discover that the first-century Roman world was quite a bit like our own. The articles indicated by the "you are there" symbol will take you to places that you may never have "visited" before. Sometimes there's also information about what life was like for the people who lived there.

A Closer Look

Sometimes the best way to understand a text of Scripture is to **compare** the text to a related passage and/or its connected article. That's why you'll find symbols that "advertise" companion passages and articles that provide insight into the passage indicated.

Quote Unquote

Occasionally you might be interested in knowing what someone else besides the writers of Scripture had to say about an idea raised in the biblical text, or about the text itself. That's not to suggest that these **quotations** from various authors are on a par with Scripture. But one way to gain perspective on the implications of a passage is to read what someone has written, and then use that to reflect on what God has said.

THEMES TO CONSIDER

In designing The Word In Life Study Bible, the editors wanted to create a resource that would help people deal with the issues of today, not yesterday. To that end, they identified a number of themes to highlight. Articles and other information provide a starting point for thought, study, and discussion of the following important areas:

WORK

For most of us, work is the most dominating area of life. It determines where we'll live, what kind of lifestyle we'll have, even who our friends will be. Yet how many of us are aware of how much the Bible says about work and workplace issues?

ECONOMICS

Who can doubt the importance of economic issues in a world increasingly tied together in a giant global marketplace? Of course, Scripture wasn't written to be an economics textbook. Nevertheless, it gives us principles relating to wealth, money, value, service, the environment, and other topics affecting both public policy and personal financial decisions.

ETHICS

This is the issue of right and wrong, of integrity and character. In a day when truth and values have become relative, we need to return to God's unchanging Word as our absolute standard for ethical conduct and commitments.

ETHNICITY

One has only to glance at a map of our modern world to recognize the impact of racial and ethnic differences. The landscape is strewn with wars, conflicts, and problems tied to long-standing ethnic tensions. How should Christians respond, especially living in an increasingly pluralistic society? As the early church discovered, the gospel has enormous implications for how we relate to others from different backgrounds.

THE CHURCH

Enormous opportunities and critical choices face the church today. A fresh look at the church's beginnings and its impact on the first-century world can offer valuable guidelines for the church's impact on the twenty-first-century world.

LAITY

Elton Trueblood has pointed out that the first Reformation put the Word of God back into the hands of the people of God; now we face the prospect of a "second reformation" that can put the *work* of God back into the hands of the people of God. This means that "everyday" believers can participate in carrying out God's work and find meaning and value in their efforts.

THE FAMILY

Building marriages and families that honor God has perhaps never been harder than today. That's why *The Word In Life Study Bible* highlights passages, principles, and people that show us the fundamental truths—and the honest realities—of building healthy family relationships in a fallen world.

THE CITY

Today for the first time in history, more people live in metropolitan than in rural areas. That has enormous implications for how Christians engage the world. Yet many believers have adopted a negative view of the city; some even see it as an evil. But when we read the Bible, we discover that the gospel "conquered" the Roman world by penetrating its major cities. The same thing can happen today.

WITNESS

One thing is certain about evangelism: both non-Christians and Christians feel uncomfortable with it. Yet Jesus has sent His followers into the world to communicate His message of salvation. Fortunately, the Bible gives us guidelines for carrying out the task in a way that is winsome, sensitive, and effective.

WOMEN

One of the most significant developments in recent culture has been the growing awareness of and sensitivity to issues and concerns of women—their dignity, their needs, and their rights. *The Word In Life Study Bible* places a special emphasis on the many women of the Scriptures and their significant contribution to the ministry of Jesus and the growth of the church. It also highlights the condition of women in the ancient world and the biblical teaching that pertains to the lives of women both then and now.

The themes mentioned above are just some of the ones that are touched on. It wouldn't be possible to classify them all. But as you use The Word In Life Study Bible, *it will stir up your thinking and show you other areas in which to apply God's word to life.* ◆

HOW TO USE THE SYMBOL SYSTEM

The section above concerning 'Features to Look For' mentions four symbols that are used to designate various kinds of articles, tables, or related material in The Word In Life Study Bible.

From time to time as you read the biblical text, you will see one of those four symbols along the left side of the text, accompanied by a box containing information that will lead you to a feature that has to do with the biblical passage you are reading.

If the feature you are being sent to is on one of the two pages you are opened to (called a 'spread'), then the box next to the symbol by the text will contain just chapter-and-verse information, designating one verse (for example, 1:10) or a range of verses (1:1–16). No page number is given. Just look on the spread you are opened to for a matching symbol accompanied by a box

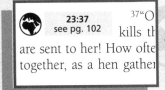

> 1:1–16
> ¹The Christ
> Abraham:
> ²Abraham begot Isaac,

containing the name of the symbol (such as CONSIDER THIS) and matching chapter-and-verse information.

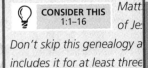

> CONSIDER THIS
> 1:1–16
> Matt.
> of Je:
> Don't skip this genealogy a
> includes it for at least three

If the feature you are being sent to is someplace other than the spread you are opened to, then the box next to the symbol by the text will contain chapter-and-verse information and a page number. Just look on the designated page for a matching symbol accompanied by a box containing the name of the symbol and matching chapter-and-verse information.

> 23:37
> see pg. 102
> ³⁷"O kills th
> are sent to her! How ofte
> together, as a hen gathe

> YOU ARE THERE
> 23:37
> • Mai
> Pale
> biblical times.
> • Well-situated for d

NEW KING JAMES FOOTNOTES

> your brethren*a* only, what do you do more *than* not even the tax collectors*b* do so? [48]Therefore

As you read, you will often see a raised letter in the biblical text. Each raised letter designates a New King James footnote, to be found at the foot of the text. Each footnote is designated by the chapter and verse in which its raised letter is contained. Then you will see the raised letter, followed by the footnote. (The letter *a* is used for the first footnote connected to each verse. If a verse has more than one footnote connected to it, then the second footnote receives the letter *b*. The chapter and verse are not repeated in such cases.)

New King James footnotes contain helpful information about significant textual variations and alternate translations, as well as some explanations and references to other passages of Scripture.

Footnotes concerning textual variations make no evaluation of readings, but do clearly indicate the manuscript sources of readings. They objectively present the facts without such remarks as 'the best manuscripts omit' or 'the most reliable manuscripts read,' which are value judgments that differ according to varying viewpoints on the text.

Where significant variations occur in the New Testament Greek manuscripts, textual notes are classified as followed:

❶ NU-Text

These variations from the traditional text represent the text as published in the twenty-sixth edition of the Nestle-Aland Greek New Testament (N) and in the United Bible Societies' third edition (U), hence the abbreviation, 'NU-Text.'

Example:

> As we forgive our debtors.
> *6:4 ªNU-Text omits openly.   6:6 ªNU-Text omits openly.*

❷ M-Text

These variations from the traditional text represent the Majority Text, which is based on the majority of surviving manuscripts. It should be noted that M stands for whatever reading is printed in the first edition of *The Greek New Testament According to the Majority Text,* whether supported by overwhelming, strong, or only a divided majority textual tradition.

Example:

> be baptized by him. [14]And John *tried to* prevent
> *3:11 ªM-Text omits and fire.*

The textual notes reflect the scholarship of the past 150 years and will assist the reader to observe the variations between the different manuscript traditions of the New Testament. Such information is generally not available in English translations of the New Testament.

✦ ✦

OTHER FEATURES

MAPS

Many maps appear throughout The Word In Life Study Bible. They are designed to provide relevant geographical information in an accessible and easy-to-read format, on the same pages with the biblical text and related features.

A number of locator maps show you quickly where a certain place is with regard to its surrounding area.

CHORAZIN
A city condemned by Christ for not repenting.

Sidon

Capernaum • • Bethsaida

GALILEE

Nazareth •

Sea of Galilee

Caesarea •

Mediterranean Sea

SAMARIA

DECAPOLIS

Jordan River

Joppa •

THE TWELVE

Apostle	Description
Simon (Peter) (Mark 1:16)	Fisherman from Galilee, Andrew's brother
Andrew (John 1:40)	Fisherman from Galilee, Peter's brother
James	Son of Zebedee, brother to John; from Capernaum
John (Introduction to John)	Son of Zebedee, brother to James; from Capernaum
Philip	From Bethsaida
Bartholomew	From Cana in Galilee

TABLES

Information is often presented in the form of tables or lists, showing at a glance how various facts and ideas relate to each other.

The Gospel Explained

What does it mean to be a Christian? Do you know? Many people today who call themselves Christians would be hard pressed to explain the term. Some would talk in generalities about "doing good." Others would say that Christianity means love. Others would say it means "following Jesus," though they have only the vaguest idea of what they are talking about.

Every Christian ought to read the book of Romans. It was written to explain the faith. While the first five books of the New Testament tell the story of Jesus, Romans examines the *message* of Jesus. It shows that His gospel is far more than just nice feelings or high moral sentiments. It is truth. It has intellectual content. It makes a difference in the way people think, and therefore in what they believe.

Romans

The gospel is more than high moral sentiments. It is truth.

C O N T E N T S

Do Not Avenge Yourself (12:19–21)

Romans says vengeance belongs to God. What, then, can you do to those who hurt you?

The High Calling of Government Service (13:6)

If you work in government, you'll want to pay special attention to this article.

Are Sundays Special? (14:5–13)

Should Sunday be treated as a special day in light of God's instructions regarding a Sabbath?

Paul's Female Coworkers (16:1)

Not a few of Paul's most valued associates were women, several of whom are listed in Romans 16.

Who Was Paul's Mother? (16:13)

Meet a woman who played such an important role in Paul's life that he never forgot her.

WHY DID JESUS DIE?

In Romans we find a carefully constructed argument that answers a crucial question: *Why did Jesus die?* The author, Paul, used his training as a Pharisee in writing this letter. As a rabbi, a teacher of the Law, he knew how to dissect theological issues and philosophical questions. In Romans he works his way through a sophisticated argument, not unlike a modern-day lawyer writing a brief. He asks and answers question after question until he has finished constructing a body of material that hangs together logically and theologically.

Romans shows that the gospel is big enough to deal with the weighty issues of the world—earth's ecology, ethical tensions arising from technology, world wars, humanity's capacity for self-destruction, human dignity, justice. Not everyone needs to look at Christianity on such a scale, but the great thinkers do. Romans does not disappoint: it offers the *big* picture of God's salvation.

This book may not be the easiest reading, but it is profoundly rewarding. Among the peaks of Scripture it looms like the Himalayas; its climax, chapter 8, towers up like Mount Everest. Scaling these vistas will give anyone's mental faculties a real workout—but the view is incomparable! Those who read and study Romans gain a grand perspective on what it means to be a Christian. They no longer have to guess at what the gospel is all about—they *know.* ◆

THE SUPER-POWERFUL GOSPEL

We know almost nothing about the people to whom Romans was sent. Although Paul mentions the church at Rome (1:7), he wrote a general letter to a general readership, as if addressing it "to whom it may concern." Paul didn't start the church at Rome, nor had he ever visited there before writing this letter (1:13–15). In fact, he even intended to push beyond Rome to Spain (15:22–24).

But even if we know little about Paul's Roman readers, we know much about first-century Rome (see Acts 28:16). Rome was the greatest superpower of its day. Its influence extended from Britain to Africa and from Spain to Persia. This vast empire was governed very effectively by provincial heads, petty kings, and vassals of Rome. A pax Romana (Roman peace) and a superior road system facilitated transportation and commerce and enabled the rapid spread of Christianity.

Overall, Rome's government, economy, infrastructure, and defense were formidable enough to last for a thousand years. The Romans were a people in love with power. Perhaps that's why Paul described the gospel to the believers there in terms of power—God's power to save (Rom. 1:16). It's a gospel powerful enough to handle the empire, big enough to address issues on a global scale.

The salvation described in this book extends to . . .

- all aspects of life. *The gospel is not just personal or private, but public and universal as well. It deals with nations, with public policy, with science and technology, with race relations, with good and evil, with the cosmos, with the architecture of the world system.*

- all times and places. *Romans describes the grand sweep of history, from creation to Christ to the culmination of the world. At every point, God is carrying out His strategy for saving His creation from sin.*

- all kinds of people. *Jews and Gentiles, men and women, powerful and powerless, good and bad—all have a place in God's salvation story.*

Rome treated its Caesars like gods and gave them dominion over numerous territories and peoples. But the book of Romans affirms Christ as supreme Lord over all creation: over the past (chapters 3–5), over the present (chapters 6–8), over nations (chapters 9–11), and over daily living in a complex society (chapters 12–16). Christ is even Lord over the environment (chapter 8). Corrupted as it is and languishing under the crushing domination of Adam's sin, the world yearns for redemption. Fortunately, Adam's power to corrupt is exceeded by Christ's power to restore.

Overall, Romans presents a message for public people to embrace. The gospel is about God's power for anyone who lives and works in public systems and institutions. Is your faith big enough for the issues and tasks you face in your work and your world? If you're a marketplace Christian, Romans is a "must-read." ◆

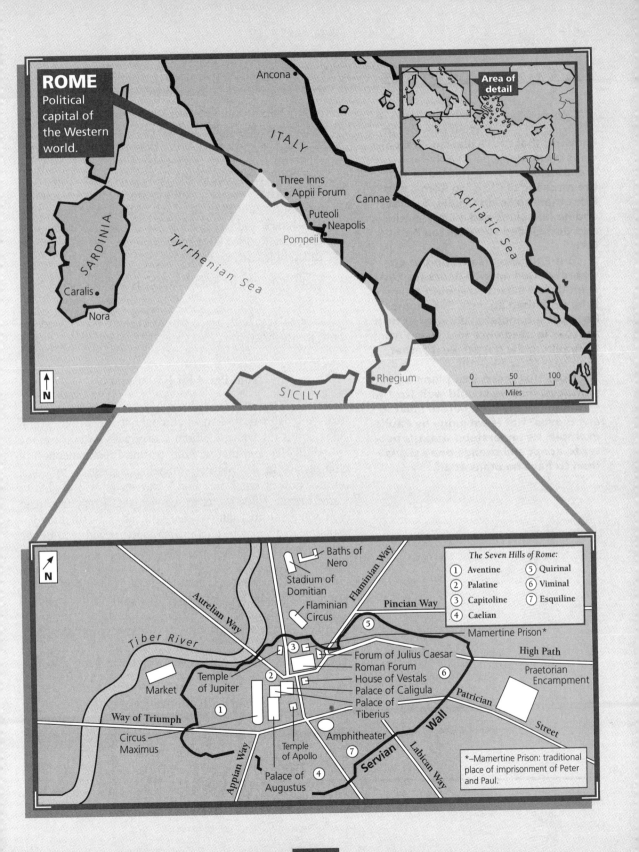

ROME

Political capital of the Western world.

Ancona

ITALY

Area of detail

Three Inns
Appii Forum
Cannae
Puteoli
Neapolis
Pompeii

SARDINIA

Adriatic Sea

Tyrrhenian Sea

Caralis
Nora

Rhegium

SICILY

0   50   100
Miles

N

N

Baths of Nero

Stadium of Domitian

Flaminian Circus

Flaminian Way

Aurelian Way

Pincian Way

Tiber River

The Seven Hills of Rome:
① Aventine ⑤ Quirinal
② Palatine ⑥ Viminal
③ Capitoline ⑦ Esquiline
④ Caelian

Mamertine Prison*

High Path

Praetorian Encampment

Forum of Julius Caesar
Roman Forum
House of Vestals
Palace of Caligula
Palace of Tiberius

Temple of Jupiter

Market

②

③

⑤

⑥

①

Way of Triumph

Patrician Street

Circus Maximus

Amphitheater

⑦

Servian Wall

Labican Way

Temple of Apollo

Appian Way

Palace of Augustus

④

*–Mamertine Prison: traditional place of imprisonment of Peter and Paul.

A CHANGE OF PLANS

💡 **CONSIDER THIS** **Somehow there's a**
1:13 **certain comfort in**
knowing that Paul's plans did not always work out (v. 13). Paul was a
great visionary. He intended to take
the message of Christ to Rome, and
from there to Spain (15:28). To that
end he laid plans and made decisions,
and God guided and directed his efforts.

But Paul was also willing to go
wherever God opened doors for him,
even if that meant scrapping a carefully organized agenda. For example,
he made a complete, 180-degree turn
at Troas in obedience to a vision from
God, taking the gospel west rather
than east (Acts 16:6–10).

Does that mean that planning is
pointless, that we should wait for the
"leading" of the Lord before making
any moves? Not if we judge by Paul's
example. He understood that it's better to adapt and change one's plans
than to have no plans at all.

*Paul felt driven to get to Rome, but Spain was just as
significant. See "All Roads Lead to Rome—and Beyond,"
Acts 28:28–31.*

CHAPTER 1

Greetings

[1]Paul, a bondservant of Jesus Christ, called *to be* an apostle, separated to the gospel of God [2]which He promised before through His prophets in the Holy Scriptures, [3]concern-
ing His Son Jesus Christ our Lord, who was born of the
seed of David according to the flesh, [4]*and* declared *to be* the
Son of God with power according to the Spirit of holiness,
by the resurrection from the dead. [5]Through Him we have
received grace and apostleship for obedience to the faith
among all nations for His name, [6]among whom you also are
the called of Jesus Christ;

[7]To all who are in Rome, beloved of God, called *to be*
saints:

Grace to you and peace from God our Father and the
Lord Jesus Christ.

Paul Prays for His Readers

[8]First, I thank my God through Jesus Christ for you all,
that your faith is spoken of throughout the whole world.
[9]For God is my witness, whom I serve with my spirit in the
gospel of His Son, that without ceasing I make mention of
you always in my prayers, [10]making request if, by some
means, now at last I may find a way in the will of God to
come to you. [11]For I long to see you, that I may impart to
you some spiritual gift, so that you may be established—
[12]that is, that I may be encouraged together with you by the
mutual faith both of you and me.

💡 **1:13** [13]Now I do not want you to be un-
aware, brethren, that I often planned to
come to you (but was hindered until now), that I might
have some fruit among you also, just as among the other
Gentiles. [14]I am a debtor both to Greeks and to barbarians,
both to wise and to unwise. [15]So, as much as is in me, *I am*
ready to preach the gospel to you who are in Rome also.

The Gospel Is the Power of God

💡 **1:16** [16]For I am not ashamed of the gospel
of Christ,[a] for it is the power of God to
salvation for everyone who believes, for the Jew first and
also for the Greek. [17]For in it the righ-
💡 **1:17**
see pg. 538 teousness of God is revealed from faith to
faith; as it is written, "The just shall live by faith."[a]

1:16 [a]NU-Text omits *of Christ*.   *1:17* [a]Habakkuk 2:4

God Will Judge Sin

[18]For the wrath of God is revealed from heaven against all ungodliness and unrighteousness of men, who suppress the truth in unrighteousness, [19]because what may be known of God is manifest in them, for God has shown *it* to them. [20]For since the creation of the world His invisible *attributes* are clearly seen, being understood by the things that are made, *even* His eternal power and Godhead, so that they are without excuse, [21]because, although they knew God, they did not glorify *Him* as God, nor were thankful, but became futile in their thoughts, and their foolish hearts were darkened. [22]Professing to be wise, they became fools, [23]and changed the glory of the incorruptible God into an image made like corruptible man—and birds and four-footed animals and creeping things.

[24]Therefore God also gave them up to uncleanness, in the lusts of their hearts, to dishonor their bodies among themselves, [25]who exchanged the truth of God for the lie, and worshiped and served the creature rather than the Creator, who is blessed forever. Amen.

[26]For this reason God gave them up to vile passions. For even their women exchanged the natural use for what is against nature. [27]Likewise also the men, leaving the natural use of the woman, burned in their lust for one another, men with men committing what is shameful, and receiving in themselves the penalty of their error which was due.

[28]And even as they did not like to retain God in *their* knowledge, God gave them over to a debased mind, to do those things which are not fitting; [29]being filled with all unrighteousness, sexual immorality,[a] wickedness, covetousness, maliciousness; full of envy, murder, strife, deceit, evilmindedness; *they are* whisperers, [30]backbiters, haters of God, violent, proud, boasters, inventors of evil things, disobedient to parents, [31]undiscerning, untrustworthy, unloving, unforgiving,[a] unmerciful; [32]who, knowing the righteous judgment of God, that those who practice such things are deserving of death, not only do the same but also approve of those who practice them.

CHAPTER 2

All Are Guilty, Whether Jew or Gentile

[1]Therefore you are inexcusable, O man, whoever you are who judge, for in whatever you judge another you condemn yourself; for you who judge practice the same things. [2]But we know that the judgment of God is according to truth against those who practice such things. [3]And do you think this, O man, you who judge those practicing such

1:29 [a]NU-Text omits sexual immorality. 1:31 [a]NU-Text omits unforgiving.

THE POWER OF THE GOSPEL

CONSIDER THIS 1:16 **Are you ever embarrassed to be identified as a follower of Christ? Would coworkers or other associates ever assume that you are ashamed of your faith by the way you avoid talking about it or revealing your true thoughts and feelings?**

Paul felt no shame in the message of Christ, for he saw it as *powerful*— powerful enough to transform lives (v. 16).

How powerful is the gospel you believe in? Are you a channel or a barrier for the power of Christ in your workplace?

The first followers of Jesus experienced the power of the gospel in such a profound way that they changed the entire Roman world. See "Power," Acts 1:8.

things, and doing the same, that you will escape the judgment of God? [4]Or do you despise the riches of His goodness, forbearance, and longsuffering, not knowing that the goodness of God leads you to repentance? [5]But in accordance with your hardness and your impenitent heart you are treasuring up for yourself wrath in the day of wrath and revelation of the righteous judgment of God, [6]who "will render to each one according to his deeds":[a] [7]eternal life to those who by patient continuance in doing good seek for glory, honor, and immortality; [8]but to those who are self-seeking and do not obey the truth, but obey unrighteousness—indignation and wrath, [9]tribulation and anguish, on every soul of man who does evil, of the Jew first and also of the Greek; [10]but glory, honor, and peace to everyone who works what is good, to the Jew first and also to the Greek. [11]For there is no partiality with God.

2:6 [a]Psalm 62:12; Proverbs 24:12

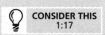

CONSIDER THIS
1:17

RIGHTEOUSNESS

One of the greatest challenges confronting believers today is to communicate the message of Christ in terms that everyday people can understand. Words like "righteousness" (v. 17) have become unrecognizable to many in our culture, and even to many in the church.

Yet it's hard to talk about the gospel—and virtually impossible to understand Romans—without coming to terms with the word "righteousness" (Greek, dikaiosune). In fact, the New Testament uses the term in one form or another no less than 228 times, at least 40 in Romans. What, then, does "righteousness" mean and how does the gospel reveal "the righteousness of God" (v. 17)?

The word "righteous" goes back to a base, reg, meaning "move in a straight line." Thus, "righteous" (rightwise) means "in the straight (or right) way." Used with reference to morality, "righteous" means living or acting in the right way.

But what is the "right" way? In our society, people commonly say that everyone must determine what is right for oneself. However, Scripture offers a different standard—indeed, the ultimate standard of rightness or "righteousness," God Himself. God's character reveals what is absolutely right. He is the measure of moral right and wrong.

He is also the source of right living. It's important to understand that righteousness involves more than just determining whether or not one has lived up to the perfect standard that God sets. The fact is, no one has except Je-

🔍 **2:12**
see pg. 540

¹²For as many as have sinned without law will also perish without law, and as many as have sinned in the law will be judged by the law ¹³(for not the hearers of the law *are* just in the sight of God, but the doers of the law will be justified; ¹⁴for when Gentiles, who do not have the law, by nature do the things in the law, these, although not having the law, are a law to themselves, ¹⁵who show the work of the law written in their hearts, their conscience also bearing witness, and between themselves *their* thoughts accusing or else excusing *them)* ¹⁶in the day when God will judge the secrets of men by Jesus Christ, according to my gospel.

Being Jewish Is Not Enough

¹⁷Indeed[a] you are called a Jew, and rest on the law, and make your boast in God, ¹⁸and know *His* will, and approve

2:17 [a]NU-Text reads *But if.*

---

sus (Rom. 3:23; 5:18–21). Thus, in a legal sense, all of us stand guilty before God. We are all "unrighteous." We have all "sinned" (literally, "missed the mark").

But the message of Romans is that God has done and is doing everything that needs to be done to restore things to the way He originally intended—to the right *way.* For example, He dealt with sin through Jesus' death on the cross (5:6–11), and He transfers the righteousness of Christ to those who trust in Him (5:1–2). As believers, we can enjoy a restored relationship with God.

That means that we can begin to live with righteousness, *that is,* in a way that pleases God and fulfills His purposes for us. We can do that because He gives us the ability to do it (8:1–17). Rather than trying to "prove" ourselves good enough for Him or live up to impossible moral standards, we can relate to Him in love, expecting Him to help us as we make choices about how to live.

The gospel, then, is "good news" because it reveals God's right *way.* It tells us that He is a good God who, in love and mercy, has done something about the wrong *way* that the world has taken. How have you responded to that good news of God's righteousness? ◆

Another term that is often misunderstood today is gospel. *To learn more about what it means, see "What Is the Gospel?" Luke 7:22.*

GOD WILL JUDGE THE SECRETS OF MEN BY JESUS CHRIST. . . .
—Romans 2:16

the things that are excellent, being instructed out of the law, [19]and are confident that you yourself are a guide to the blind, a light to those who are in darkness, [20]an instructor of the foolish, a teacher of babes, having the form of knowledge and truth in the law. [21]You, therefore, who teach another, do you not teach yourself? You who preach that a man should not steal, do you steal? [22]You who say, "Do not commit adultery," do you commit adultery? You who abhor idols, do you rob temples? [23]You who make your boast in the law, do you dishonor God through breaking the law? [24]For "the name of God is blasphemed among the Gentiles because of you,"[a] as it is written.

[25]For circumcision is indeed profitable if you keep the law; but if you are a breaker of the law, your circumcision has become uncircumcision. [26]Therefore, if an uncircumcised man keeps the righteous requirements of the law, will not his uncircumcision be counted as circumcision? [27]And will not the physically uncircumcised, if he fulfills the law, judge you who, *even with your* written *code* and circumci-

2:24 [a]Isaiah 52:5; Ezekiel 36:22

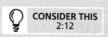

CONSIDER THIS
2:12

THE LAW

Paul's reference to "law" (v. 12) has to do not with laws in general, but with the specific code of rules and regulations that God gave to Moses on Mount Sinai. The Law was part of the covenant that set Israel apart as God's people. It governed their worship, their relationship to God, and their social relationships with one another. The Ten Commandments form a summary of that Law.

Israel was not the only nation to have a law code. Indeed, such collections were common in the ancient world. Most of them began by explaining that the gods gave the king power to reign, along with a pronouncement about how good and capable he was. Then came the king's laws grouped by subject. Finally, most of the codes closed with a series of curses and blessings.

What set the Mosaic Law apart from these other codes was, first of all, its origin. The Law was given by God Himself. It issued from His very nature; like Him it was holy, righteous, and good. Thus, all crimes in Israel were crimes against God (1 Sam. 12:9–10). He expected all of the people to love and serve Him (Amos 5:21–24). As their final judge, He disciplined those who violated the Law (Ex. 22:21–24; Deut. 10:18; 19:17), though He also held the nation responsible for insuring that justice was carried out (Deut. 13:6–10; 17:7; Num. 15:32–36).

Furthermore, God ruled over Israel, in effect, as the

sion, *are* a transgressor of the law? ²⁸For he is not a Jew who *is one* outwardly, nor *is* circumcision that which *is* outward in the flesh; ²⁹but *he is* a Jew who *is one* inwardly; and circumcision *is that* of the heart, in the Spirit, not in the letter; whose praise *is* not from men but from God.

CHAPTER 3

Faith Alone Makes Heritage Valuable

¹What advantage then has the Jew, or what *is* the profit of circumcision? ²Much in every way! Chiefly because to them were committed the oracles of God. ³For what if some did not believe? Will their unbelief make the faithfulness of God without effect? ⁴Certainly not! Indeed, let God be true but every man a liar. As it is written:

> "That You may be justified in Your words,
>   And may overcome when You are judged."^a

3:4 ^aPsalm 51:4

nation's King. Ancient kings often enacted laws to try to outdo their predecessors in image, economic power, and political influence. God, however, gave His law as an expression of love for His people, to advance their best interests (Ex. 19:5–6).

The Law can be divided into three categories— moral laws, ceremonial laws, and civil laws. The latter regulated in great detail matters having to do with leaders, the army, criminal cases, crimes against property, humane treatment, personal and family rights, property rights, and other social behavior.

The ceremonial laws contained specifications regarding public worship and ritual, giving high priority to the concept of holiness. Because God is holy (Lev. 21:8), Israel was to be holy in all its religious practices.

The Law was given specifically to Israel, but it rests on eternal moral principles that are consistent with God's character. Thus it is a summary of fundamental and universal moral standards. It expresses the essence of what God requires of people. That's why when God judges, He can be impartial. Gentiles will not be judged by the Law (Rom. 2:12), since it was not given to them, but they will still be judged by the same righteous standard that underlies the Law. ◆

LET GOD BE TRUE BUT EVERY MAN A LIAR.
—Romans 3:4

NOBODY'S PERFECT

**CONSIDER THIS
3:9–18** It's common today for people to excuse their faults with the attitude, "Hey, nobody's perfect!" True enough. People can only be expected to be human—and that means fallible.

Unfortunately, though, few people take that reality seriously enough. Indeed, when it comes to their standing before God, all too many take a different stance: they may not be perfect, but they're "good enough."

The question is, are they good enough for God? Romans 3 says they are not. That's what Paul means when he writes, "all are under sin" (v. 9) and then cites a number of Old Testament passages to back up his claim (vv. 10–18).

It's not that people are evil through and through, or that they never do any moral good. Quite the contrary. People are capable of impressive acts of courage, compassion, and justice. But in light of God's holy (morally perfect) character, which is the ultimate standard against which people's goodness is measured, people are indeed far from perfect. Their good behavior turns out to be the exception rather than the rule.

The good news that Paul writes about in Romans, however, is that God has reached out to humanity despite its imperfect ways. His attitude has not been one of rejection, as if to say, "They're not good enough for Me," but one of grace and compassion that says, in effect, "I will make them into good people—people as good as I AM—by means of Christ My Son."

Another popular notion today is that humankind is basically good, and that moral problems are simply the result of bad parenting, bad education, and the foibles of "society." Is that true? See "Are People Basically Good?" Rom. 7:21.

⁵But if our unrighteousness demonstrates the righteousness of God, what shall we say? *Is* God unjust who inflicts wrath? (I speak as a man.) ⁶Certainly not! For then how will God judge the world?

⁷For if the truth of God has increased through my lie to His glory, why am I also still judged as a sinner? ⁸And *why* not *say,* "Let us do evil that good may come"?—as we are slanderously reported and as some affirm that we say. Their condemnation is just.

All Stand Condemned before God

3:9–18 ⁹What then? Are we better *than they?* Not at all. For we have previously charged both Jews and Greeks that they are all under sin.
¹⁰As it is written:

"There is none righteous, no, not one;
11 There is none who understands;
   There is none who seeks after God.
12 They have all turned aside;
   They have together become unprofitable;
   There is none who does good, no, not one."ᵃ
13 "Their throat *is* an open tomb;
   With their tongues they have practiced deceit";ᵃ
   "The poison of asps *is* under their lips";ᵇ
14 "Whose mouth *is* full of cursing and bitterness."ᵃ
15 "Their feet *are* swift to shed blood;
16 Destruction and misery *are* in their ways;
17 And the way of peace they have not known."ᵃ
18 "There is no fear of God before their eyes."ᵃ

¹⁹Now we know that whatever the law says, it says to those who are under the law, that every mouth may be stopped, and all the world may become guilty before God. ²⁰Therefore by the deeds of the law no flesh will be justified in His sight, for by the law *is* the knowledge of sin.

The Way of Righteousness—By Faith

²¹But now the righteousness of God apart from the law is revealed, being witnessed by the Law and the Prophets, ²²even the righteousness of God, through faith in Jesus Christ, to all and on allᵃ who believe. For there is no difference; ²³for all have sinned and fall short of the glory of God, ²⁴being justified freely by His grace through the redemption that is in Christ Jesus, ²⁵whom God set forth *as* a propitiation by His blood, through faith, to demonstrate His righteousness, because in His forbearance God had passed over the sins that were previously committed, ²⁶to demonstrate

3:12 ᵃPsalms 14:1–3; 53:1–3; Ecclesiastes 7:20   *3:13* ᵃPsalm 5:9   ᵇPsalm 140:3   *3:14* ᵃPsalm 10:7   *3:17* ᵃIsaiah 59:7, 8   *3:18* ᵃPsalm 36:1   *3:22* ᵃNU-Text omits *and on all.*

at the present time His righteousness, that He might be just and the justifier of the one who has faith in Jesus.

²⁷Where *is* boasting then? It is excluded. By what law? Of works? No, but by the law of faith. ²⁸Therefore we conclude that a man is justified by faith apart from the deeds of the law. ²⁹Or is *He* the God of the Jews only? *Is He* not also the God of the Gentiles? Yes, of the Gentiles also, ³⁰since *there is* one God who will justify the circumcised by faith and the uncircumcised through faith. ³¹Do we then make void the law through faith? Certainly not! On the contrary, we establish the law.

CHAPTER 4

Abraham Was Justified by Faith

¹What then shall we say that Abraham our father has found according to the flesh?ᵃ ²For if Abraham was justified by works, he has *something* to boast about, but not before God. ³For what does the Scripture say? "Abraham believed God, and it was accounted to him for righteousness."ᵃ ⁴Now to him who works, the wages are not counted as grace but as debt.

⁵But to him who does not work but believes on Him who justifies the ungodly, his faith is accounted for righteousness, ⁶just as David also describes the blessedness of the man to whom God imputes righteousness apart from works:

7   "Blessed *are those* whose lawless deeds are forgiven,
    And whose sins are covered;

8   Blessed *is the* man to whom the LORD shall not impute sin."ᵃ

⁹*Does* this blessedness then *come* upon the circumcised *only,* or upon the uncircumcised also? For we say that faith was accounted to Abraham for righteousness. ¹⁰How then was it accounted? While he was circumcised, or uncircumcised? Not while circumcised, but while uncircumcised. ¹¹And he received the sign of circumcision, a seal of the righteousness of the faith which *he had while still* uncircumcised, that he might be the father of all those who believe, though they are uncircumcised, that righteousness might be imputed to them also, ¹²and the father of circumcision to those who not only *are* of the circumcision, but who also walk in the steps of the faith which our father Abraham *had while still* uncircumcised.

¹³For the promise that he would be the heir of the world *was* not to Abraham or to his seed through the law, but

4:1 ᵃOr *Abraham our (fore)father according to the flesh has found?*   4:3 ᵃGenesis 15:6
4:8 ᵃPsalm 32:1, 2

ABRAHAM

CONSIDER THIS
4:1

As father of the Hebrews, Abraham (v. 1) features prominently in the New Testament. Here in Romans 4, he is recalled as an individual. Elsewhere he represents the entire people of Israel, and especially those who have placed faith in God (for example, 9:7; 11:1; Gal. 3:6–9).

Indeed, Abraham's faith is what makes him so important to the New Testament writers. God made important promises to him and his descendents, Isaac, Jacob, and Jacob's twelve sons—promises that God repeated throughout Israel's history. Abraham is remembered as the man who believed that God would do what He said He would do (Rom. 4:3)—a remarkable thing when we consider that at the time of the promises, Abraham had very little evidence that God would follow through, certainly far less than the New Testament writers or we who live today.

One of the most important promises was that God would send a Messiah, an "anointed one." Jesus claimed to be that Messiah. So the central question of the New Testament becomes, do we believe that? Do we take Jesus at His word? Do we accept His claim and its implications? Abraham believed God; do we?

Another important question raised by the coming of Jesus was, what happens to Israel? Even though many Jews believed Jesus' claims and followed Him, by and large the nation rejected Him. What did that mean for the promises of God? Paul deals with those issues in Romans 9–11 (see "Israel," Rom. 10:1).

DAVID

💡 **CONSIDER THIS**
4:6
If Abraham (v. 1) was honored as the patriarch of Israel, David (v. 6) was honored as the king of Israel. He was not the nation's first king, but He was God's choice for king (1 Sam. 16:1–13).

If anyone might have a claim on being right with God and meriting His favor, then, it was David. After all, he was said to be a man after God's own heart (13:14; Acts 13:22). Furthermore, God established a covenant with him, promising that his heirs would have a right to the throne of Israel forever (2 Sam. 7:12; 22:51). He was even a direct ancestor of Jesus Christ (Matt. 1:6; Luke 3:31).

But David relied on none of these advantages (or "works," Rom. 4:5) when it came to his standing before God. Instead, he threw himself on God's mercy, trusting in His gracious character to forgive his sin and establish his "righteousness" (v. 6), or right standing in relation to God. Psalm 32, from which Romans 4:7–8 quotes, celebrates this delivery from sin that God brings about.

Do you rely on your own good works to establish your relationship with God? Romans 4 says you can never be good enough. That's why God offers an alternative—trusting in Jesus' righteousness to cover your sin and make it possible for you to know God.

It's virtually impossible to understand Romans without coming to terms with the word "righteousness." Learn more about what that word means at Rom. 1:17.

---

through the righteousness of faith. [14]For if those who are of the law *are* heirs, faith is made void and the promise made of no effect, [15]because the law brings about wrath; for where there is no law *there is* no transgression.

God Rewarded Abraham's Faith

💡 **4:16–25**
[16]Therefore *it is* of faith that *it might be* according to grace, so that the promise might be sure to all the seed, not only to those who are of the law, but also to those who are of the faith of Abraham, who is the father of us all [17](as it is written, "I have made you a father of many nations"[a]) in the presence of Him whom he believed—God, who gives life to the dead and calls those things which do not exist as though they did; [18]who, contrary to hope, in hope believed, so that he became the father of many nations, according to what was spoken, "So shall your descendants be."[a] [19]And not being weak in faith, he did not consider his own body, already dead (since he was about a hundred years old), and the deadness of Sarah's womb. [20]He did not waver at the promise of God through unbelief, but was strengthened in faith, giving glory to God, [21]and being fully convinced that what He had promised He was also able to perform. [22]And therefore "it was accounted to him for righteousness."[a]

[23]Now it was not written for his sake alone that it was imputed to him, [24]but also for us. It shall be imputed to us who believe in Him who raised up Jesus our Lord from the dead, [25]who was delivered up because of our offenses, and was raised because of our justification.

CHAPTER 5

Through Faith We Have Peace with God

[1]Therefore, having been justified by faith, we have[a] peace with God through our Lord Jesus Christ, [2]through whom also we have access by faith into this grace in which we stand, and rejoice in hope of the glory of God. [3]And not only *that*, but we also glory in tribulations, knowing that tribulation produces perseverance; [4]and perseverance, character; and character, hope. [5]Now hope does not disappoint, because the love of God has been poured out in our hearts by the Holy Spirit who was given to us.

[6]For when we were still without strength, in due time Christ died for the ungodly. [7]For scarcely for a righteous man will one die; yet perhaps for a good man someone would even dare to die. [8]But God demonstrates His own love toward us, in that while we were still sinners, Christ

---

4:17 [a]Genesis 17:5   **4:18** [a]Genesis 15:5   **4:22** [a]Genesis 15:6   **5:1** [a]Another ancient reading is, *let us have peace.*

died for us. [9]Much more then, having now been justified by His blood, we shall be saved from wrath through Him. [10]For if when we were enemies we were reconciled to God through the death of His Son, much more, having been reconciled, we shall be saved by His life. [11]And not only *that*, but we also rejoice in God through our Lord Jesus Christ, through whom we have now received the reconciliation.

Through Faith Christ Makes Us Alive Again

[12]Therefore, just as through one man sin entered the world, and death through sin, and thus death spread to all men, because all sinned— [13](For until the law sin was in the world, but sin is not imputed when there is no law.

✓ 5:14 [14]Nevertheless death reigned from Adam to Moses, even over those who had not sinned according to the likeness of the transgression of Adam, who is a type of Him who was to come. [15]But the free gift *is* not like the offense. For if by the one man's offense many died, much more the grace of God and the gift by the grace of the one Man, Jesus Christ, abounded to many. [16]And the gift *is* not like *that which came* through the one who sinned. For the judgment *which came* from one *offense resulted* in condemnation, but the free gift *which came* from many offenses *resulted* in justification. [17]For if by the one man's offense death reigned through the one, much more those who receive abundance of grace and of the gift of righteousness will reign in life through the One, Jesus Christ.)

[18]Therefore, as through one man's offense *judgment* came to all men, resulting in condemnation, even so through one Man's righteous act *the free gift came* to all men, resulting in justification of life. [19]For as by one man's disobedience many were made sinners, so also by one Man's obedience many will be made righteous.

[20]Moreover the law entered that the offense might abound. But where sin abounded, grace abounded much more, [21]so that as sin reigned in death, even so grace might reign through righteousness to eternal life through Jesus Christ our Lord.

CHAPTER 6

Through Faith We Can Obey God

[1]What shall we say then? Shall we continue in sin that grace may abound? [2]Certainly not! How shall we who died to sin live any longer in it? [3]Or do you not know that as many of us as were baptized into Christ Jesus were baptized

(Bible text continued on page 547)

PROMISES

💡 CONSIDER THIS 4:16–25 **Do you believe that God can be depended on to honor His promises? Abraham did (vv. 20–21).**

All of us rely on the promises of others in our daily lives and work. Vendors promise to deliver products in specified quantities and qualities. Project groups promise to deliver results by certain dates. Companies promise to stand behind their products with "satisfaction guaranteed." If we can believe the promises of fallible human beings, how much more can we trust the promises of God, who never fails?

Of course, if we are one of God's people, we need to live and work with the same trustworthiness and reliability. When we give our word, we need to fulfill it. When we make a commitment, we need to honor it. When we enter into a contract, we need to abide by it. Otherwise, we bring discredit to God.

◆ ◆ ◆ ◆ ◆ ◆ ◆ ◆ ◆ ◆ ◆ ◆ ◆ ◆ ◆ ◆ ◆ ◆ ◆

Trustworthiness is one of the traits of a godly "workstyle." See Titus 2:9–10.

ADAM

✓ FOR YOUR INFO 5:14 **Adam (v. 14) was the first man, who, along with his wife, Eve, was created by God on the sixth day of creation and placed in the Garden of Eden (Gen. 1:26–28; 2:7–24). Thus they became the ancestors of all humanity.**

But Adam failed to keep God's command not to eat the fruit of a certain tree in the garden, resulting in a dramatic change—indeed, a tragic rupture—in the relationship between God and Adam and Eve and their descendants. His choice to disobey brought sin and death into the world (Rom. 5:12–19; 1 Cor. 15:22).

SLAVES

Paul uses a powerful image when he pictures one's relationship either to sin or to obedience as slavery (v. 16). The Roman Empire was heavily dependent on slaves to take care of its hard labor and menial tasks. In fact, many of Paul's Roman recipients may have been slaves, since perhaps half the population or more were under servitude by one historian's estimate.

Slaves were taken from the many nations that Rome conquered. Those assigned to the empire's widespread construction projects or to its mines had a hard lot. Fed a subsistence diet, they were worked to exhaustion. Injuries and disease were common, and once they were too sick to work, or in rare cases too old, they were abandoned.

Household slaves, however, enjoyed better conditions. Nearly every Roman home owned at least two or three servants, and some had hundreds. They assisted the women in maintaining their homes and raising their children. Slaves with occupational expertise proved particularly valuable in the workplace, and some businesses were entirely dependent on these imported, cheap laborers.

Slavery existed long before the Romans, of course. The Bible records several different forms of slavery in ancient times: domestic slavery, as illustrated by Hagar (Gen. 16:1); state slavery, as illustrated by the Israelites under Egypt (Ex. 5:6–19; 13:3); and temple slavery, as illustrated by the slaves of the Levites for temple service (Num. 31:25–47; Josh. 9:21–27).

Curiously, the Bible does not directly condemn slavery as an institution, though it contains warnings about the practice of slavery (Amos 1:6–9; Rev. 18:13). The Old Testament Law did regulate Israel's treatment of slaves (Ex. 21; Deut. 15). Repeatedly, the people were instructed not to rule over a fellow Israelite harshly (Lev. 25:39; Deut. 15:14). If a master beat a slave or harmed him, the law provided that the slave could go free (Ex. 21:26–27); and the killing of a slave called for a penalty (Ex. 21:20).

In the New Testament, slaves were advised to obey their masters (Eph. 6:5; Col. 3:22; Titus 2:9). Paul appealed to Philemon to receive back Onesimus, a runaway slave who became a Christian and therefore a brother (see the Introduction to Philemon). This was an illustration that in Christ, social distinctions such as slavery no longer apply (Gal. 3:28; Col. 3:11). Elsewhere Paul counseled believing slaves to seek freedom if they could (1 Cor. 7:21).

Under Jewish law, no Hebrew was to be the permanent slave of another Hebrew (Ex. 21:2; Lev. 25:37–43; Deut. 15:12). If a slave desired to continue with his master, he would have a mark made in the ear to signify that he had chosen to remain a slave (Ex. 21:5–6). A slave could also buy his freedom, or another person could buy his freedom for him (Lev. 25:47–49).

Among the Romans, an owner could free a slave outright, or the slave could purchase his freedom by paying his owner. Freedom could also be arranged if ownership was transferred to a god. The slave could then receive his freedom in return for contracting his services. He would continue with his master, but now as a free man.

Perhaps Paul had that sort of arrangement in mind when he described the moral choice of which master one would obey—sin or righteousness (Rom. 6:16). For as believers, we have been freed from sin, and in fact are now owned by God. We are now free to serve God. Yet we still have a choice to serve either sin or God. In light of the realities of slavery, it's worth considering: Which master are you serving? Which one is likely to treat you better? ◆

into His death? ⁴Therefore we were buried with Him through baptism into death, that just as Christ was raised from the dead by the glory of the Father, even so we also should walk in newness of life.

⁵For if we have been united together in the likeness of His death, certainly we also shall be *in the likeness* of *His* resurrection, ⁶knowing this, that our old man was crucified with *Him,* that the body of sin might be done away with, that we should no longer be slaves of sin. ⁷For he who has died has been freed from sin. ⁸Now if we died with Christ, we believe that we shall also live with Him, ⁹knowing that Christ, having been raised from the dead, dies no more. Death no longer has dominion over Him. ¹⁰For *the death* that He died, He died to sin once for all; but *the life* that He lives, He lives to God. ¹¹Likewise you also, reckon yourselves to be dead indeed to sin, but alive to God in Christ Jesus our Lord.

¹²Therefore do not let sin reign in your mortal body, that you should obey it in its lusts. ¹³And do not present your members *as* instruments of unrighteousness to sin, but present yourselves to God as being alive from the dead, and your members *as* instruments of righteousness to God. ¹⁴For sin shall not have dominion over you, for you are not under law but under grace.

We Are No Longer Enslaved to Sin

6:15–22

6:16

¹⁵What then? Shall we sin because we are not under law but under grace? Certainly not! ¹⁶Do you not know that to whom you present yourselves slaves to obey, you are that one's slaves whom you obey, whether of sin *leading* to death, or of obedience *leading* to righteousness? ¹⁷But God be thanked that *though* you were slaves of sin, yet you obeyed from the heart that form of doctrine to which you were delivered. ¹⁸And having been set free from sin, you became slaves of righteousness. ¹⁹I speak in human *terms* because of the weakness of your flesh. For just as you presented your members *as* slaves of uncleanness, and of lawlessness *leading* to *more* lawlessness, so now present your members *as* slaves *of* righteousness for holiness.

²⁰For when you were slaves of sin, you were free in regard to righteousness. ²¹What fruit did you have then in the things of which you are now ashamed? For the end of those things *is* death. ²²But now having been set free from sin, and having become slaves of God, you have your fruit to holiness, and the end, everlasting life. ²³For the wages of sin *is* death, but the gift of God *is* eternal life in Christ Jesus our Lord.

REAL FREEDOM

CONSIDER THIS
6:15–22

One of the greatest motivating factors for people throughout the world today is the quest for freedom, for self-determination. Armies fight for it. Nations vote for it. Individuals work for it.

But here in Romans 6, Scripture teaches that, ultimately, no one is ever totally "free." In the end, everyone serves either God or sin. In fact, Paul uses the word "slaves" to describe the relationship (vv. 16–20; see related article on "Slaves"). We are either slaves of righteousness or slaves of sin.

What does that imply for our understanding of the nature of freedom? Is complete autonomy possible? Is there such a thing as self-rule or political self-determination? Yes, in a limited sense. But here as elsewhere, Scripture describes real freedom as a change of masters: being set free from slavery to sin in order to become slaves to righteousness instead.

All of us are enslaved to sin from the moment of conception. Our only hope is Christ, who is able to emancipate us from that bondage (7:24–25). Then, having saved us, He enables us through His Holy Spirit to do what we could not do in and of ourselves—live in obedience to God's law (8:3–4). Therein lies true freedom.

CHAPTER 7

A New View of the Law

¹Or do you not know, brethren (for I speak to those who know the law), that the law has dominion over a man as long as he lives? ²For the woman who has a husband is bound by the law to *her* husband as long as he lives. But if the husband dies, she is released from the law of *her* husband. ³So then if, while *her* husband lives, she marries another man, she will be called an adulteress; but if her husband dies, she is free from that law, so that she is no adulteress, though she has married another man. ⁴Therefore, my brethren, you also have become dead to the law through the body of Christ, that you may be married to another—to Him who was raised from the dead, that we should bear fruit to God. ⁵For when we were in the flesh, the sinful passions which were aroused by the law were at work in our members to bear fruit to death. ⁶But now we have been delivered from the law, having died to what we

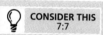

CONSIDER THIS
7:7

SCYLLA AND CHARYBDIS

Ancient Greek mythology told of two dangers at sea known as Scylla and Charybdis. Scylla was a twelve-tentacled monster with six heads that grabbed at least six sailors from the decks of passing ships. Nearby lay Charybdis, an underwater terror able to suck down entire vessels in a giant whirlpool of seawater. These two dangers were arranged so that a ship could sail closer to one or the other, but could avoid neither.

The Christian life has two dangers not unlike Scylla and Charybdis. As believers travel along the journey of faith, they encounter two perils that cannot be avoided—law and lawlessness. Paul addresses both pitfalls in Romans 6–7.

In Romans, the Law (7:7; see 2:12) refers specifically to the Old Testament Law that God gave to Israel, but more generally to the moral expectations that God places on all humanity. Obviously such standards are not evil in themselves. Nevertheless, they become perilous because no one is humanly able to keep them all perfectly.

Paul illustrated that fact by citing the Tenth Commandment, "You shall not covet" (7:7; Ex. 20:17). That was a basic moral principle with which Paul was in total agreement. Yet when he examined his own life, he found "all manner of evil desire." In other words, the more Paul understood God's Law, the more aware he became of the sin in his life. Nor did knowing God's expectations make him

were held by, so that we should serve in the newness of the Spirit and not *in* the oldness of the letter.

7:7 ⁷What shall we say then? *Is the law sin?* Certainly not! On the contrary, I would not have known sin except through the law. For I would not have known covetousness unless the law had said, "You shall not covet."ᵃ ⁸But sin, taking opportunity by the commandment, produced in me all *manner of* evil desire. For apart from the law sin *was* dead. ⁹I was alive once without the law, but when the commandment came, sin revived and I died. ¹⁰And the commandment, which *was* to *bring* life, I found to *bring* death. ¹¹For sin, taking occasion by the commandment, deceived me, and by it killed *me.* ¹²Therefore the law *is* holy, and the commandment holy and just and good.

A Terrible Inner Conflict

¹³Has then what is good become death to me? Certainly not! But sin, that it might appear sin, was producing death

7:7 ᵃExodus 20:17; Deuteronomy 5:21

capable of doing them. In fact, he found himself incapable of carrying them out (v. 19).

The end result was frustration and wretchedness (v. 24). How many Christians today feel similarly? They are keenly aware of the expectations of the Christian life, yet they are also aware of how poorly they carry out those expectations. As a result, they feel guilt and condemnation. So they become preoccupied with doing acts of morality rather than with the person of Christ. Such an attitude is called legalism.

However, if an overemphasis on law is perilous, its opposite, lawlessness, is just as perilous. Scripture says that all sin is lawlessness (6:19; 1 John 3:4), because to sin is to violate God's law, His moral expectations. But one sinful act has a way of spawning another, and yet another, until things snowball into a lifestyle of lawlessness. Some Christians end up in that condition—especially many who have previously suffered under legalism.

Scylla and Charybdis were myths of the Greeks, but the perils of law and lawlessness are no illusions. They are real dangers that Christians face every day. There is only one way to avoid either pitfall: Christ must produce in us the good that we cannot produce through our own human ability (8:1–4). If we want to fulfill the expectations of God, we must rely on the power of God to enable us to do so. Are you trusting Christ to reproduce His character in you? ◆

SERVE IN THE NEWNESS OF THE SPIRIT AND NOT IN THE OLDNESS OF THE LETTER.
—Romans 7:6

ARE PEOPLE BASICALLY GOOD?

💡 **CONSIDER THIS**
7:21
Many of us want to believe that we are "basically good" people—or at least better than other people. In fact, it's popular today to subscribe to the view that humankind is basically good, and that moral problems are simply the result of bad parenting, bad education, and the foibles of "society."

The Bible presents a different view, however. Scripture affirms the inherent dignity and value of every human being (Ps. 139:13–14; see "People At Work," Heb. 2:7). But it insists that each of us is born "in sin"—that is, apart from God, naturally tending toward wrong rather than right. That's what Paul addresses in Romans 7.

Original sin is a sobering concept, one that our pride would dearly love to do away with. But then, pride lies at the root of sin. Therefore, the first step toward rooting it out of our lives is to humbly admit our true condition—not to blame someone else, but rather to confess our sin to God and trust solely in His grace for forgiveness and acceptance (Luke 18:13).

This attitude of humility in light of our sin needs to become a way of life. Sin is so deeply entrenched within us that we can never safely say that we've mastered it (1 Cor. 4:4; 10:12). Instead, we live with limitation, admitting that we don't have all the answers to our own problems, let alone those that plague the world.

This perspective provides insight into the troubles that come our way. Sometimes they come as a result of our own sinful choices. Sometimes

(continued on next page)

in me through what is good, so that sin through the commandment might become exceedingly sinful. [14]For we know that the law is spiritual, but I am carnal, sold under sin. [15]For what I am doing, I do not understand. For what I will to do, that I do not practice; but what I hate, that I do. [16]If, then, I do what I will not to do, I agree with the law that *it is* good. [17]But now, *it is* no longer I who do it, but sin that dwells in me. [18]For I know that in me (that is, in my flesh) nothing good dwells; for to will is present with me, but *how* to perform what is good I do not find. [19]For the good that I will *to do,* I do not do; but the evil I will not *to do,* that I practice. [20]Now if I do what I will not *to do,* it is no longer I who do it, but sin that dwells in me.

💡 **7:21**   [21]I find then a law, that evil is present with me, the one who wills to do good. [22]For I delight in the law of God according to the inward man. [23]But I see another law in my members, warring against the law of my mind, and bringing me into captivity to the law of sin which is in my members. [24]O wretched man that I am! Who will deliver me from this body of death? [25]I thank God—through Jesus Christ our Lord

So then, with the mind I myself serve the law of God, but with the flesh the law of sin.

CHAPTER 8

In Christ There Is No More Condemnation

[1]There is therefore now no condemnation to those who are in Christ Jesus,[a] who do not walk according to the flesh, but according to the Spirit. [2]For the law of the Spirit of life in Christ Jesus has made me free from the law of sin and death. [3]For what the law could not do in that it was weak through the flesh, God *did* by sending His own Son in the likeness of sinful flesh, on account of sin: He condemned sin in the flesh, [4]that the righteous requirement of the law might be fulfilled in us who do not walk according to the flesh but according to the Spirit. [5]For those who live according to the flesh set their minds on the things of the flesh, but those *who live* according to the Spirit, the things of the Spirit. [6]For to be carnally minded *is* death, but to be spiritually minded *is* life and peace. [7]Because the carnal mind *is* enmity against God; for it is not subject to the law of God, nor indeed can be. [8]So then, those who are in the flesh cannot please God.

Believers Are People of the Spirit

[9]But you are not in the flesh but in the Spirit, if indeed the Spirit of God dwells in you. Now if anyone does not

8:1 [a]NU-Text omits the rest of this verse.

have the Spirit of Christ, he is not His. ¹⁰And if Christ *is* in you, the body *is* dead because of sin, but the Spirit *is* life because of righteousness. ¹¹But if the Spirit of Him who raised Jesus from the dead dwells in you, He who raised Christ from the dead will also give life to your mortal bodies through His Spirit who dwells in you.

¹²Therefore, brethren, we are debtors—not to the flesh, to live according to the flesh. ¹³For if you live according to the flesh you will die; but if by the Spirit you put to death the deeds of the body, you will live. ¹⁴For as many as are led by the Spirit of God, these are sons of God.

8:15–17 ¹⁵For you did not receive the spirit of bondage again to fear, but you received the Spirit of adoption by whom we cry out, "Abba, Father." ¹⁶The Spirit Himself bears witness with our spirit that we are children of God, ¹⁷and if children, then heirs—heirs of God and joint heirs with Christ, if indeed we suffer with *Him*, that we may also be glorified together.

Believers Receive the Spirit's Help

¹⁸For I consider that the sufferings of this present time are not worthy *to be compared* with the glory which shall be revealed in us. ¹⁹For the earnest expectation of the creation eagerly waits for the revealing of the sons

8:20 see pg. 552 of God. ²⁰For the creation was subjected to futility, not willingly, but because of Him who subjected

8:21–22 see pg. 554 it in hope; ²¹because the creation itself also will be delivered from the bondage of corruption into the glorious liberty of the children of God. ²²For we know that the whole creation groans and labors with birth pangs together until now. ²³Not only *that,* but we also who have the firstfruits of the Spirit, even we ourselves groan within ourselves, eagerly waiting for the adoption, the redemption of our body. ²⁴For we were saved in this hope, but hope that is seen is not hope; for why does one still hope for what he sees? ²⁵But if we hope for what we do not see, we eagerly wait for *it* with perseverance.

²⁶Likewise the Spirit also helps in our weaknesses. For we do not know what we should pray for as we ought, but the Spirit Himself makes intercession for us[a] with groanings which cannot be uttered. ²⁷Now He who searches the hearts

(Bible text continued on page 553)

8:26 [a]NU-Text omits *for us.*

An Inheritance?

A CLOSER LOOK 8:15–17 *As God's adopted children, believers are promised an inheritance (vv. 15–17). What will that involve? See "What's In It for Me?" Eph. 1:11.*

(continued from previous page)

God allows them as a way of building our character, especially our faith in Him (Ps. 119:67, 71–72; Heb. 12:7–11; James 1:2–4, 12–18).

Do you want true humility? It comes from seeing yourself in relation to God. See "Humility—The Scandalous Virtue," Phil. 2:3.

To Be Spiritually Minded Is Life And Peace.
—Romans 8:6

IS WORK A CURSE?

What was the curse that God put on creation (v. 20)? One of the most stubborn myths in Western culture is that God imposed work as a curse to punish Adam and Eve's sin (Gen. 3:1–19). As a result, some people view work as something evil. Scripture does not support that idea:

God Himself is a worker. The fact that God works shows that work is not evil, since by definition God cannot do evil. On the contrary, work is an activity that God carries out. See "God: The Original Worker," John 5:17.

God created people in His image to be His coworkers. He gives us ability and authority to manage His creation. See "People At Work," Heb. 2:7.

God established work before the fall. Genesis 1–2 record how God created the world. The account tells how He placed the first humans in a garden "to tend and keep it" (2:15). This work assignment was given before sin entered the world and God pronounced the curse (Gen. 3). Obviously, then, work cannot be a result of the fall since people were working before the fall.

God commends work even after the fall. If work were evil in and

of itself, God would never encourage people to engage in it. But He does. For example, He told Noah and his family the same thing He told Adam and Eve—to have dominion over the earth (Gen. 9:1–7). In the New Testament, Christians are commanded to work (Col. 3:23; 1 Thess. 4:11).

Work itself was not cursed in the fall. A careful reading of Genesis 3:17–19 shows that God cursed the *ground* as a result of Adam's sin—but not work:

"Cursed is the ground for
   your sake;
In toil you shall eat of it
All the days of your life.
Both thorns and thistles it
   shall bring forth for you,
And you shall eat the herb of
   the field.
In the sweat of your face you
   shall eat bread
Till you return to the ground,
For out of it you were taken;

For dust you are,
And to dust you shall return."

Notice three ways that this curse affected work: (1) Work had been a joy, but now it would be "toil." People would feel burdened down by it, and even come to hate it. (2) "Thorns and thistles" would hamper people's efforts to exercise dominion. In other words, the earth would not be as cooperative as it had been. (3) People would have to "sweat" to accomplish their tasks. Work would require enormous effort and energy.

Most of us know all too well how burdensome work can be. Workplace stresses and pressures, occupational hazards, the daily grind, office politics, crushing boredom, endless routine, disappointments, setbacks, catastrophes, frustration, cutthroat competition, fraud, deception, injustice—there is no end of evils connected with work. But work itself is not evil. Far from naming it a curse, the Bible calls work and its fruit a gift from God (Eccl. 3:13; 5:18–19). ◆

Do you know that your job is actually an extension of Christ's rule over the world? See "People at Work," Heb. 2:7.

knows what the mind of the Spirit *is,* because He makes intercession for the saints according to *the will of* God.

⨀ **8:28** ²⁸And we know that all things work together for good to those who love God, to those who are the called according to *His* purpose. ²⁹For whom He foreknew, He also predestined *to be* conformed to the image of His Son, that He might be the firstborn among many brethren. ³⁰Moreover whom He predestined, these He also called; whom He called, these He also justified; and whom He justified, these He also glorified.

Believers Are Loved by God

³¹What then shall we say to these things? If God *is* for us, who *can be* against us? ³²He who did not spare His own Son, but delivered Him up for us all, how shall He not with Him also freely give us all things? ³³Who shall bring a charge against God's elect? *It is* God who justifies. ³⁴Who *is* he who condemns? *It is* Christ who died, and furthermore is also risen, who is even at the right hand of God, who also makes intercession for us. ³⁵Who shall separate us from the love of Christ? *Shall* tribulation, or distress, or persecution, or famine, or nakedness, or peril, or sword? ³⁶As it is written:

"For Your sake we are killed all day long;
 We are accounted as sheep for the slaughter."ᵃ

³⁷Yet in all these things we are more than conquerors through Him who loved us. ³⁸For I am persuaded that neither death nor life, nor angels nor principalities nor powers, nor things present nor things to come, ³⁹nor height nor depth, nor any other created thing, shall be able to separate us from the love of God which is in Christ Jesus our Lord.

CHAPTER 9

The Implications of Faith for Israel

☑ **9:1 see pg. 556** ¹I tell the truth in Christ, I am not lying, my conscience also bearing me witness in the Holy Spirit, ²that I have great sorrow and continual grief in my heart. ³For I could wish that I myself were accursed from Christ for my brethren, my countrymenᵃ according to the flesh, ⁴who are Israelites, to whom *pertain* the adoption, the glory, the covenants, the giving of the law, the service *of God,* and the promises; ⁵of whom *are* the fathers and from whom, according to the flesh, Christ *came,* who is over all, *the* eternally blessed God. Amen.

8:36 ᵃPsalm 44:22   9:3 ᵃOr relatives

ALL THINGS FOR GOOD?

⨀ **CONSIDER THIS 8:28** Verse 28 is easy to quote to someone else. But what about when it's *your* turn to suffer? Is there comfort in this passage? Notice two important things as you consider Paul's words here:

(1) All things work together *for* good but not all things *are* good. The loss of a job, a tyrannical boss, physical illness, or family troubles are not good *per se.* In fact, often they are the direct result of evil. That's important to observe. Believers are never promised immunity from the problems and pains of the world. Every day we must put up with much that is not good.

(2) Nevertheless, good can come out of bad! This verse promises that God uses all the circumstances of our lives—both the good and the bad—to shape outcomes that accomplish His purposes for us. And His purposes can only be good, because He is good by definition (James 1:17).

So how can you make this verse work for you as you face tough, troubling times?

- **Affirm your trust in God's presence.**
- **Align your goals with God's purposes.**
- **Accept the reliability of God's promises.**

⁶But it is not that the word of God has taken no effect. For they *are* not all Israel who *are* of Israel, ⁷nor *are they* all children because they are the seed of Abraham; but, "In Isaac your seed shall be called."*ᵃ* ⁸That is, those who *are* the children of the flesh, these *are* not the children of God; but the children of the promise are counted as the seed. ⁹For this *is* the word of promise: "At this time I will come and Sarah shall have a son."*ᵃ*

¹⁰And not only *this,* but when Rebecca also had conceived by one man, *even* by our father Isaac ¹¹(for *the children* not yet being born, nor having done any good or evil, that the purpose of God according to election might stand, not of works but of Him who calls), ¹²it was said to her, "The older shall serve the younger."*ᵃ* ¹³As it is written, "Jacob I have loved, but Esau I have hated."*ᵃ*

God Is Sovereign

¹⁴What shall we say then? *Is there* unrighteousness with God? Certainly not! ¹⁵For He says to Moses, "I will have mercy on whomever I will have mercy, and I will have com-

9:7 ᵃGenesis 21:12   9:9 ᵃGenesis 18:10, 14   9:12 ᵃGenesis 25:23   9:13 ᵃMalachi 1:2, 3

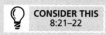

CONSIDER THIS
8:21–22

THE LIBERATION OF CREATION

I n Romans 8, Paul painted on a cosmic canvas a vast picture of the world, from its origin as God's beautiful creation to the impact of sin, and on to its ultimate restoration at the end of history. If you've ever wondered what's ultimately going to happen to the world, if you've ever worried about environmental disaster, if you've ever wished that evil could somehow be vanquished, this passage is "must reading."

Paul recognized that the world is both delightful and disastrous, orderly and chaotic. He offered a good news/bad news scenario. The bad news is that all of creation, including human beings and their environments, are corrupted by sin. Sin is so prevalent and so destructive that we need more than just a better earth—we need a new earth. Sin is not just personal, it's global. It's infused in the bloodstream of the whole world, where sinful people create systems and cultures that promote and protect evil, as well as good.

So much for the bad news. The good news is that God's salvation is equally universal in its availability and effects. His saving grace starts its work inside people, but eventually works its way out through their influence. God's power and purposes begin to penetrate their values,

passion on whomever I will have compassion."*a* 16So then *it is* not of him who wills, nor of him who runs, but of God who shows mercy. 17For the Scripture says to the Pharaoh, "For this very purpose I have raised you up, that I may show My power in you, and that My name may be declared in all the earth."*a* 18Therefore He has mercy on whom He wills, and whom He wills He hardens.

19You will say to me then, "Why does He still find fault? For who has resisted His will?" 20But indeed, O man, who are you to reply against God? Will the thing formed say to him who formed *it*, "Why have you made me like this?" 21Does not the potter have power over the clay, from the same lump to make one vessel for honor and another for dishonor?

22*What* if God, wanting to show *His* wrath and to make His power known, endured with much longsuffering the vessels of wrath prepared for destruction, 23and that He might make known the riches of His glory on the vessels of mercy, which He had prepared beforehand for glory, 24*even* us whom He called, not of the Jews only, but also of the Gentiles?

9:15 *a*Exodus 33:19   9:17 *a*Exodus 9:16

worldview, relationships, career choices, and community involvements. As God's managers of the earth, they begin to reclaim the devil's territory, as it were, by redirecting social systems and cultural values so that people and places benefit instead of being exploited. What begins as personal conversion results in societal change as God's people slowly impact their families, coworkers, churches, communities, culture, and environment.

But this liberation of creation will be partial and imperfect until Christ returns to redeem it personally. In the meantime, the world groans like a woman in labor (v. 22), waiting for its delivery from sin. Christ calls His followers to participate in the world's systems, to promote His values and love as we have opportunity. As His people, we affirm both the salvation of persons and the transformation of places, participating with Him in the first skirmishes of the liberation of His creation. ◆

O MAN, WHO ARE YOU TO REPLY AGAINST GOD?
—Romans 9:20

²⁵As He says also in Hosea:

> "I will call them My people, who were not My people,
> And her beloved, who was not beloved."[a]
> ²⁶ "And it shall come to pass in the place where it was said to them,
> 'You *are* not My people,'
> There they shall be called sons of the living God."[a]

²⁷Isaiah also cries out concerning Israel:[a]

> "Though the number of the children of Israel be as the sand of the sea,
> The remnant will be saved.

9:25 ªHosea 2:23   9:26 ªHosea 1:10   9:27 ªIsaiah 10:22, 23

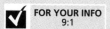

FOR YOUR INFO
9:1

GOD'S HEART FOR THE WHOLE WORLD

n Romans 9–11, Paul reminds us that God's heart reaches out to the whole world, both Jews and Gentiles:

GOOD NEWS FOR THE WORLD IN ROMANS 9–11	
Passage	**Teaching**
9:24	•God in His mercy calls not only Jews but Gentiles as well.
9:25	•Gentiles, who were not God's people, have become children of the living God.
9:30	•Gentiles have received righteousness through their faith, just as Jews who have believed in Jesus.
10:3	•But Jews who seek God through the Law's requirements will never find righteousness because they do not seek it through faith. They seek to establish their own righteousness, not God's.
10:4	•Jesus is God's righteousness to everyone who believes.
9:33; 10:9,11	•Faith in Jesus is the key to salvation.
10:12–13	•When it comes to who can be saved, God makes no distinction between Jews and Gentiles.
10:20–21; 11:11	•The Gentiles, who were not looking for God, found Him. But the Jews, whom God continually reached out to, did not want Him.
11:1–2	•God has not given up on the Jews. Many have turned to God; Paul was one of them.
11:14	•The Gentiles found Christ through the witness of the Jews. Paul's great desire was for Jews to come to Christ through the witness of the Gentiles.
11:16–24	•Gentiles were grafted into God's tree of life as Jews rejected God and were broken off. But that leaves no room for pride or arrogance on the part of the Gentiles; rather, humility.
11:19–24	•Jews were "cut off" because they refused to believe. If they repent, God is able to graft them in again.
11:32	•God's desire is to have mercy on all.

◆

By the time Paul wrote Romans, Gentiles had probably become a majority in the church. Paul saw the possibility of a church divided, and the tragedy that would result if that happened. See "Are We One People?" Rom. 11:13–24.

28 For He will finish the work and cut *it* short in
  righteousness,
  Because the LORD will make a short work upon
  the earth."*a*

29And as Isaiah said before:

"Unless the LORD of Sabaoth*a* had left us a seed,
  We would have become like Sodom,
  And we would have been made like
  Gomorrah."*b*

30What shall we say then? That Gentiles, who did
not pursue righteousness, have attained to righteousness, even the righteousness of faith; 31but Israel, pursuing the law of righteousness, has not attained to the law of righteousness.*a* 32Why? Because
they did not *seek it* by faith, but as it were, by the
works of the law.*a* For they stumbled at that stumbling stone. 33As it is written:

"Behold, I lay in Zion a stumbling stone and
  rock of offense,
  And whoever believes on Him will not be put
  to shame."*a*

CHAPTER 10

Paul Longs for Israel's Salvation

**10:1
see pg. 558** 1Brethren, my heart's desire
and prayer to God for Israel*a* is
that they may be saved. 2For I bear them witness
that they have a zeal for God, but not according to
knowledge. 3For they being ignorant of God's righteousness, and seeking to establish their own righteousness, have not submitted to the righteousness
of God. 4For Christ *is* the end of the law for righteousness to everyone who believes.

5For Moses writes about the righteousness which
is of the law, "The man who does those things shall
live by them."*a* 6But the righteousness of faith
speaks in this way, "Do not say in your heart, 'Who
will ascend into heaven?' "*a* (that is, to bring Christ
down *from above*) 7or, " 'Who will descend into the
abyss?' "*a* (that is, to bring Christ up from the

dead). 8But what does it say? "The word is near
you, in your mouth and in your heart"*a* (that is, the
word of faith which we preach): 9that if you confess with your mouth the Lord Jesus and believe in
your heart that God has raised Him from the dead,
you will be saved. 10For with the heart one believes
unto righteousness, and with the mouth confession
is made unto salvation. 11For the Scripture says,
"Whoever believes on Him will not be put to
shame."*a* 12For there is no distinction between Jew
and Greek, for the same Lord over all is rich to all
who call upon Him. 13For "whoever calls on the
name of the LORD shall be saved."*a*

The Nation Needs to Hear the Gospel

14How then shall they call on Him in whom they
have not believed? And how shall they believe in
Him of whom they have not heard? And how shall
they hear without a preacher? 15And how shall they
preach unless they are sent? As it is written:

"How beautiful are the feet of those who preach
  the gospel of peace,*a*
  Who bring glad tidings of good things!"*b*

16But they have not all obeyed the gospel. For Isaiah says, "LORD, who has believed our report?"*a*
17So then faith *comes* by hearing, and hearing by
the word of God.

18But I say, have they not heard? Yes indeed:

"Their sound has gone out to all the earth,
  And their words to the ends of the world."*a*

19But I say, did Israel not know? First Moses says:

"I will provoke you to jealousy by *those who are*
  not a nation,
  I will move you to anger by a foolish nation."*a*

20But Isaiah is very bold and says:

"I was found by those who did not seek Me;
  I was made manifest to those who did not ask
  for Me."*a*

21But to Israel he says:

"All day long I have stretched out My hands
  To a disobedient and contrary people."*a*

9:28 *a*NU-Text reads *For the LORD will finish the work and cut it short upon
the earth.*   9:29 *a*Literally, in Hebrew, *Hosts*   *b*Isaiah 1:9   9:31 *a*NU-Text
omits *of righteousness.*   9:32 *a*NU-Text reads *by works.*   9:33 *a*Isaiah 8:14;
28:16   10:1 *a*NU-Text reads *them.*   10:5 *a*Leviticus 18:5   10:6 *a*Deuteronomy
30:12   10:7 *a*Deuteronomy 30:13   10:8 *a*Deuteronomy 30:14   10:11 *a*Isaiah
28:16   10:13 *a*Joel 2:32   10:15 *a*NU-Text omits *preach the gospel of peace,
Who.*   *b*Isaiah 52:7; Nahum 1:15   10:16 *a*Isaiah 53:1   10:18 *a*Psalm 19:4
10:19 *a*Deuteronomy 32:21   10:20 *a*Isaiah 65:1   10:21 *a*Isaiah 65:2

(Bible text continued on page 559)

ISRAEL

Have you ever wondered what happened to the special relationship between God and the nation of Israel (v. 1)? Are the Jews still God's "chosen people"? Are the promises that God made to Abraham, Moses, David, and other Old Testament Hebrews still in effect? Or did God reject Israel when the nation rejected His Son, Jesus?

These are issues that Paul addresses in Romans 9–11. They are vitally important, because they relate to whether or not God is to be trusted.

Origins

God's relationship with Israel goes back thousands of years to the ancient Near East. The Bible presents Abraham (see Rom. 4:1) as the father of the nation. Abraham came from Ur, a city of ancient Sumer in Mesopotamia (Gen. 11:31), where he prospered before moving to the land of Canaan (Gen. 12:5).

There God entered into a covenant with Abraham, promising to bless his descendants and make them His special people (Gen. 12:1–3). Abraham was to remain faithful to God and to serve as a channel through which God's blessings could flow to the rest of the world.

Abraham's son Isaac had two sons, Esau and Jacob. God chose Jacob for the renewal of His promise to Abraham (Gen. 28:13–15). Jacob's name was changed to Israel after a dramatic struggle with God (Gen. 32:24–30; 35:9–15). The name Israel has been interpreted by different scholars as "prince with God," "he strives with God," "let God rule," or "God strives." The name was later applied to the descendants of Jacob through his twelve sons, the Hebrew people. These twelve tribes were called "Israelites," "children of Israel," and "house of Israel," identifying them clearly as the descendants of Israel.

God's Chosen People

God's covenant with Abraham was far more than a contract. A contract always has an end date, while a covenant, in the biblical sense, is a permanent arrangement. Furthermore, a contract generally involves only one part of a person, such as a skill, while a covenant covers a person's total being. Another striking feature is that God is holy, all-knowing, and all-powerful, yet He consented to enter into a covenant with Abraham and his descendants—weak, sinful, and imperfect as they were.

Thus, through Abraham, Israel became God's "chosen people." This covenant relationship was confirmed at Mount Sinai when the nation promised to perform "all the words which the Lord has said" (Ex. 24:3). When the people later broke their side of the agreement, they were called by their leaders to renew the covenant (2 Kin. 23:3).

God, of course, never breaks His promises, and throughout Israel's history, He has always lived up to His side of the covenant. That's why Paul can affirm that God has not "cast away" His people (Rom. 11:1). God's oath to raise up believing children to Abraham (Gen. 22:16–17) remains an "everlasting" covenant (Gen. 17:7).

This is good news for Jew and Gentile alike. For Jews it means that God has not abandoned His people. They still figure prominently in His plans and purposes. For Gentiles, it means that God is totally trustworthy. His word can be taken at face value. Are you basing your hope on the unalterable covenants of God? ◆

Because the Hebrews failed to honor their side of their covenant with God, He promised a new covenant through the prophet Jeremiah that would accomplish what the old covenant had failed to do. See "The New Covenant," 1 Cor. 11:25.

CHAPTER 11

God Has Not Given Up on His People

¹I say then, has God cast away His people? Certainly not! For I also am an Israelite, of the seed of Abraham, *of* the tribe of Benjamin. ²God has not cast away His people whom He foreknew. Or do you not know what the Scripture says of Elijah, how he pleads with God against Israel, saying, ³"LORD, they have killed Your prophets and torn down Your altars, and I alone am left, and they seek my life"? *a* ⁴But what does the divine response say to him? "I have reserved for Myself seven thousand men who have not bowed the knee to Baal."*a* ⁵Even so then, at this present time there is a remnant according to the election of grace. ⁶And if by grace, then *it is* no longer of works; otherwise grace is no longer grace.*a* But if *it is* of works, it is no longer grace; otherwise work is no longer work.

⁷What then? Israel has not obtained what it seeks; but the elect have obtained it, and the rest were blinded. ⁸Just as it is written:

> "God has given them a spirit of stupor,
> Eyes that they should not see
> And ears that they should not hear,
> To this very day."*a*

⁹And David says:

> "Let their table become a snare and a trap,
> A stumbling block and a recompense to them.
> 10   Let their eyes be darkened, so that they do not see,
> And bow down their back always."*a*

The Implications of Faith for Gentiles

¹¹I say then, have they stumbled that they should fall? Certainly not! But through their fall, to provoke them to jealousy, salvation *has come* to the Gentiles. ¹²Now if their fall *is* riches for the world, and their failure riches for the Gentiles, how much more their fullness!

11:13–24
see pg. 560

¹³For I speak to you Gentiles; inasmuch as I am an apostle to the Gentiles, I magnify my ministry, ¹⁴if by any means I may provoke to jealousy *those who are* my flesh and save some of them. ¹⁵For if their being cast away *is* the reconciling of the world, what *will* their acceptance *be* but life from the dead?

¹⁶For if the firstfruit *is* holy, the lump *is* also *holy;* and if the root *is* holy, so *are* the branches. ¹⁷And if some of the branches were broken off, and you, being a wild olive tree, were grafted in among them, and with them became a partaker of the root and fatness of the olive tree, ¹⁸do not boast against the branches. But if you do boast, *remember that* you do not support the root, but the root supports you.

¹⁹You will say then, "Branches were broken off that I might be grafted in." ²⁰Well *said.* Because of unbelief they were broken off, and you stand by faith. Do not be haughty, but fear. ²¹For if God did not spare the natural branches, He may not spare you either. ²²Therefore consider the goodness and severity of God: on those who fell, severity; but toward you, goodness,*a* if you continue in *His* goodness. Otherwise you also will be cut off. ²³And they also, if they do not continue in unbelief, will be grafted in, for God is able to graft them in again. ²⁴For if you were cut out of the olive tree which is wild by nature, and were grafted contrary to nature into a cultivated olive tree, how much more will these, who *are* natural *branches,* be grafted into their own olive tree?

Israel Will Eventually Be Saved

²⁵For I do not desire, brethren, that you should be ignorant of this mystery, lest you should be wise in your own opinion, that blindness in part has happened to Israel until the fullness of the Gentiles has come in. ²⁶And so all Israel will be saved,*a* as it is written:

> "The Deliverer will come out of Zion,
> And He will turn away ungodliness from Jacob;
> 27   For this *is* My covenant with them,
> When I take away their sins."*a*

²⁸Concerning the gospel *they are* enemies for your sake, but concerning the election *they are* beloved for the sake of the fathers. ²⁹For the gifts and the calling of God *are* irrevocable. ³⁰For as you were once disobedient to God, yet have now obtained mercy through their disobedience, ³¹even so these also have now been disobedient, that through the mercy shown you they also may obtain mercy.

11:3 *a*1 Kings 19:10, 14   11:4 *a*1 Kings 19:18   11:6 *a*NU-Text omits the rest of this verse.   11:8 *a*Deuteronomy 29:4; Isaiah 29:10   11:10 *a*Psalm 69:22, 23   11:22 *a*NU-Text adds *of God.*   11:26 *a*Or *delivered*   11:27 *a*Isaiah 59:20, 21

³²For God has committed them all to disobedience, that He might have mercy on all.

Paul's Prayer of Praise

³³Oh, the depth of the riches both of the wisdom and knowledge of God! How unsearchable *are* His judgments and His ways past finding out!

³⁴ "For who has known the mind of the LORD?
 Or who has become His counselor?"ᵃ
³⁵ "Or who has first given to Him
 And it shall be repaid to him?"ᵃ

³⁶For of Him and through Him and to Him *are* all things, to whom *be* glory forever. Amen.

CHAPTER 12

The Believer's Relationship to God

¹I beseech you therefore, brethren, by the mercies of God, that you present your bodies a living sacrifice, holy, accept-

11:34 ᵃIsaiah 40:13; Jeremiah 23:18   11:35 ᵃJob 41:11

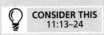

CONSIDER THIS
11:13–24

ARE WE ONE PEOPLE?

By the time Paul wrote his letter to the Christians at Rome, Gentiles were probably becoming a majority of believers throughout the church. Jews had less and less influence theologically, culturally, or politically. Gradually—and tragically—the attitudes of pride and prejudice with which Jews had looked down on Gentiles were coming back to haunt them, as Gentile believers began to turn away from their Jewish brothers.

In Romans 9–11, Paul pleaded with his Gentile readers to remember that God has not forgotten Israel. God made promises to the nation that He cannot forsake (11:29). Furthermore, Gentiles have no room for arrogance: they were not originally included among God's people, but were allowed in, like branches grafted onto a tree (vv. 17–18).

Paul saw the possibility of a church divided, with Jewish and Gentile believers going their separate ways. If that happened, Gentiles would ignore the Jewish community altogether rather than show compassion and communicate the gospel so that Jews could be saved. That's why here, as elsewhere, Paul challenged believers to pursue unity in the body of Christ and charity among the peoples of the world.

able to God, *which is* your reasonable service. ²And do not be conformed to this world, but be transformed by the renewing of your mind, that you may prove what *is* that good and acceptable and perfect will of God.

The Believer's Position in the Body of Christ

12:3
see pg. 562

³For I say, through the grace given to me, to everyone who is among you, not to think *of himself* more highly than he ought to think, but to think soberly, as God has dealt to each one a measure of faith. ⁴For as we have many members in one body, but all the members do not have the same function, ⁵so we, *being many,* are one body in Christ, and individually members of one another. ⁶Having then gifts differing according to the grace that is given to us, *let us use them:* if prophecy, *let us prophesy* in proportion to our faith; ⁷or ministry, *let us use it*

12:8

in *our* ministering; he who teaches, in teaching; ⁸he who exhorts, in exhortation; he who gives, with liberality; he who leads, with diligence; he who shows mercy, with cheerfulness.

⁹*Let* love *be* without hypocrisy. Abhor what is evil. Cling to what is good. ¹⁰*Be* kindly affectionate to one another with

* • • • • • • • • • • • • • • • •

Are we as believers today carrying out that exhortation? Unfortunately, the legacy that we've inherited is not encouraging. Had the church wholeheartedly embraced Paul's teaching, it would not have kept its tragic silence or participated in some of the great evils of the past 2,000 years. In fact, many of them probably could have been avoided, or at least resisted, had Christians paid careful attention to Romans 9–11.

We need to ask: What are the current challenges to the ethnic, racial, and cultural attitudes of believers? What tragic evils are currently operating that we need to be aware of and actively resisting? God's desire is clear—to have mercy on all (v. 32). Does that describe our heart? ◆

Paul was at pains to show that God's love and mercy extended to the whole world, both Jews and Gentiles. See how Paul accomplished that in Romans 9–11 by looking at the table, "God's Heart for the Whole World," Rom. 9:1.

QUOTE UNQUOTE

CONSIDER THIS
12:8

If God has given you the capacity to give, give liberally (v. 8):

We make a living by what we get.
We make a life by what we give.

Anonymous

brotherly love, in honor giving preference to one another; [11]not lagging in diligence, fervent in spirit, serving the Lord; [12]rejoicing in hope, patient in tribulation, continuing steadfastly in prayer; [13]distributing to the needs of the saints, given to hospitality.

The Believer's Service to the Community

[14]Bless those who persecute you; bless and do not curse. [15]Rejoice with those who rejoice, and weep with those who weep. [16]Be of the same mind toward one another. Do not set your mind on high things, but associate with the humble. Do not be wise in your own opinion.

[17]Repay no one evil for evil. Have regard for good things in the sight of all men. [18]If it is possible, as much as depends on you, live peaceably with all men. [19]Beloved, do not avenge yourselves, but *rather* give place to wrath; for it is written, "Vengeance is Mine, I will repay,"[a] says the Lord. [20]Therefore

12:19–21

> "If your enemy is hungry, feed him;
> If he is thirsty, give him a drink;

12:19 [a]Deuteronomy 32:35

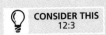

CONSIDER THIS
12:3

DO YOU SUFFER FROM "COMPARISONITIS"?

One of the most debilitating diseases of the modern world is "comparisonitis"—the tendency to measure one's worth by comparing oneself to other people. You won't find this illness listed in any of the standard medical textbooks, nor will your company's disability or health insurance or worker's compensation program reimburse you for it. But make no mistake: comparisonitis is a scourge as widespread and destructive as any physical or emotional malady known today.

Do you suffer from it? Do you find ways to look down on others and think highly of yourself because you enjoy greater abilities, intelligence, status, or wealth than they? Or do you look down on yourself and envy others because you feel you are not as capable, smart, powerful, or rich as they?

Comparisonitis is an ancient disease. Certainly Paul was aware of how deadly it could be. That's why he offered an antidote for it—to see ourselves not as we stack up against others, nor as others evaluate us, but as God sees us *(v. 3)*. Ultimately, His estimation of our worth is what matters. And to Him we matter a lot!

God does not define us according to culturally defined externals. Even our gender, ethnicity, family heritage, or

For in so doing you will heap coals of fire on his head."[a]

21Do not be overcome by evil, but overcome evil with good.

CHAPTER 13

The Believer's Submission to the State

💡 **13:1–7**
see pg. 564
1Let every soul be subject to the governing authorities. For there is no authority except from God, and the authorities that exist are appointed by God. 2Therefore whoever

💡 **13:2**
see pg. 565
resists the authority resists the ordinance of God, and those who resist will bring judgment on themselves. 3For rulers are not a terror to good works, but to evil. Do you want to be unafraid of the authority? Do what

💡 **13:4**
see pg. 564
is good, and you will have praise from the same. 4For he is God's minister to you for good. But if you do evil, be afraid; for he does not bear the sword in vain; for he is God's minister, an avenger to *execute* wrath on him who practices evil. 5Therefore *you* must

12:20 aProverbs 25:21, 22

◆ ◆ ◆ ◆ ◆ ◆ ◆ ◆ ◆ ◆ ◆ ◆ ◆ ◆ ◆

body type are not of primary importance to Him. No, He uses an altogether different set of criteria as the basis for how He deals with us, as several people in Scripture indicate:

- Paul *found that God's grace made him who he was (1 Cor. 15:10). He also discovered that despite his past, God had made him into a new person (2 Cor. 5:17).*
- Peter *learned that God's power gave him everything he needed to live his life and pursue godliness (2 Pet. 1:3).*
- Job *realized that all he had—family, friends, possessions, health—was ultimately from God (Job 1:21).*
- One of the psalmists *understood that God Himself had created him, "fearfully and wonderfully." Imagine what that did for his self-image! (Ps. 139:14).*

Do you suffer from comparisonitis? What needs to change in your self-assessment for you to see yourself as God sees you? ◆

Jesus told a parable that illustrates the deadly nature of comparisonitis. See "Comparisonitis Will Kill You," Luke 18:9–14.

DO NOT AVENGE YOURSELF

💡 **CONSIDER THIS**
12:19–21
Scripture is straightforward: no believer should avenge himself on others (v. 19). Why? Because God has reserved vengeance to Himself.

What, then, can you do to those who hurt you? You must do them good, not evil (v. 21). If you do them evil, you will yourself be overcome by evil. You can't be too careful when it comes to vengeance. One of Satan's favorite tactics is to lure someone into doing evil by providing a "good" excuse for it. And retaliation feels so appealing.

But Scripture challenges you to overcome evil, both in yourself (the will to retaliate) and in those who harm you (by doing them good). Doing so will "heap coals of fire" on the heads of your enemies (v. 20). In other words, you may magnify their sense of guilt when they see that their evil against you is met by your good toward them. Indeed, their guilty conscience may drive them to repentance.

Does Paul mean that we can never defend ourselves or our property, or that criminals should go unpunished? See "An Eye for an Eye," Matt. 5:38–42; and "The Avengers," Rom. 13:4.

THE AVENGERS

CONSIDER THIS
13:4
Governmental authorities are called by God to exact vengeance on those who do evil (v. 4). Is that inconsistent with Paul's command to believers not to avenge themselves (12:19–21)?

No, in Romans 12, Paul was addressing individuals in their private capacities. But in Romans 13, he was writing about representatives of governments in their official, public capacities. Private individuals are not to avenge themselves because God has reserved vengeance to Himself. But in doing so, God reserves the right to decide how He will bring about justice. Verse 4 indicates that one means He uses is government.

Jesus spoke along very similar lines. See "An Eye for an Eye," Matt. 5:38–42.

be subject, not only because of wrath but also for conscience' sake. [6]For because of this you also pay taxes, for they are God's ministers attending continually to this very thing. [7]Render therefore to all their due: taxes to whom taxes *are due*, customs to whom customs, fear to whom fear, honor to whom honor.

13:6
see pg. 566

The Believer's Conduct

13:8
see pg. 567

[8]Owe no one anything except to love one another, for he who loves another has fulfilled the law. [9]For the commandments, "You shall not commit adultery," "You shall not murder," "You shall not steal," "You shall not bear false witness,"[a] "You shall not covet,"[b] and if *there is* any other commandment, are *all* summed up in this saying, namely, "You shall love your neighbor as yourself."[c] [10]Love does no harm to a neighbor; therefore love *is* the fulfillment of the law.

[11]And *do* this, knowing the time, that now *it is* high time to awake out of sleep; for now our salvation is nearer than when we *first* believed. [12]The night is far spent, the day is at hand. Therefore let us cast off the works of darkness, and let us put on the armor of light. [13]Let us walk properly, as in

13:9 [a]NU-Text omits *"You shall not bear false witness."* [b]Exodus 20:13–15, 17; Deuteronomy 5:17–19, 21 [c]Leviticus 19:18

CONSIDER THIS
13:1–7

THE LIMITS OF POLITICAL AUTHORITY

When Paul wrote to the Roman believers about governing authorities (v. 1), there was no question as to what authorities he had in mind— the imperial government of Rome, probably led at the time by Nero. According to this passage, even Rome's harsh, corrupt system was established by God and deserved the respect and obedience of Christians.

However, Rome's authority—and all authority—was merely delegated authority. Ultimate authority belongs to God, as Paul pointed out. But that raises a tough question for believers, then as now: If governments are subordinate to God and accountable to Him for what they do, then aren't there limits on the extent to which believers must submit to them? Aren't there times when Christians need to obey God rather than human officials? If so, shouldn't the church pay attention to whether any particular civil government is usurping God's power and undermining His purposes rather than carrying out its intended function? The early church had to wrestle with these issues.

the day, not in revelry and drunkenness, not in lewdness and lust, not in strife and envy. [14]But put on the Lord Jesus Christ, and make no provision for the flesh, to *fulfill its* lusts.

CHAPTER 14

Controversial Practices

14:1–23
see pg. 568

[1]Receive one who is weak in the faith, *but* not to disputes over doubtful things. [2]For one believes he may eat all things, but he who is weak eats *only* vegetables. [3]Let not him who eats despise him who does not eat, and let not him who does not eat judge him who eats; for God has received him. [4]Who are you to judge another's servant? To his own master he stands or falls. Indeed, he will be made to stand, for God is able to make him stand.

14:5
see pg. 566

14:5–13
see pg. 569

[5]One person esteems *one* day above another; another esteems every day *alike*. Let each be fully convinced in his own mind. [6]He who observes the day, observes *it* to the Lord;[a] and he who does not observe the day, to the Lord he does not observe *it*. He who eats, eats to the

14:6 [a]NU-Text omits the rest of this sentence.

♦ ♦ ♦ ♦ ♦ ♦ ♦ ♦ ♦ ♦ ♦ ♦ ♦ ♦ ♦ ♦ ♦

Rome's government was far more tolerant of Christians when Paul likely wrote Romans 13 than in the 90s, when John penned Revelation. Within that span of some 30 years, believers changed their view of Rome from God's "minister for good" (v. 4) to a usurper of power that deserved to fall. In fact, the book of Revelation is seen at one level as the story of Rome's fall.

Throughout church history, believers have struggled with whether to obey or resist evil governments. There are no easy answers. But one principle that Paul clearly affirms here is that government itself is intrinsically good, having been established by God. ♦

GOVERNMENTAL AUTHORITY

CONSIDER THIS
13:2

Scripture challenges us as believers to subject ourselves to whatever governments we live under (vv. 1–7). Submission to authority is never easy. Human nature tends toward resistance and even rebellion, especially if government is imposed, incompetent, and/or corrupt. But as we struggle with how to respond to the systems in which we live, this passage offers some helpful perspectives:

(1) God is the ultimate authority (v. 1). Government as an institution has been established by God to serve His purposes. God raises up and does away with leaders.

(2) Both followers and leaders are ultimately accountable to God (v. 2). Submission to human authorities reflects our submission to God's authority.

(3) God uses governments to carry out His good purposes on earth (v. 3). Without question, some governments sometimes persecute those who do good. Paul had firsthand experience with that. But in the main, it's the lawbreaker, not the law-abiding citizen, who has something to fear from government.

(4) Obedience is a matter of inner conviction as well as external law (v. 5). Our motivation to obey must go beyond fear of punishment. As believers, we serve the highest of all authorities, God Himself.

Our responses to authority tell others much about the sincerity of our commitment to Christ. See 1 Thess. 4:12; 1 Tim. 6:1; and Titus 2:9–10.

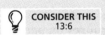

CONSIDER THIS
14:5

One modern-day believer who has become "fully convinced in his own mind" (v. 5) about Sundays has written:

It is a gross error to suppose that the Christian cause goes forward solely or chiefly on weekends. What happens on the regular weekdays may be far more important, so far as the Christian faith is concerned, than what happens on Sundays.

Elton Trueblood, *Your Other Vocation*, p. 57

Lord, for he gives God thanks; and he who does not eat, to the Lord he does not eat, and gives God thanks. [7]For none of us lives to himself, and no one dies to himself. [8]For if we live, we live to the Lord; and if we die, we die to the Lord. Therefore, whether we live or die, we are the Lord's. [9]For to this end Christ died and rose[a] and lived again, that He might be Lord of both the dead and the living. [10]But why do you judge your brother? Or why do you show contempt for your brother? For we shall all stand before the judgment seat of Christ.[a] [11]For it is written:

> "*As* I live, says the LORD,
> Every knee shall bow to Me,
> And every tongue shall confess to God."[a]

[12]So then each of us shall give account of himself to God. [13]Therefore let us not judge one another anymore, but rather resolve this, not to put a stumbling block or a cause to fall in *our* brother's way.

Pursue Peace with Each Other

[14]I know and am convinced by the Lord Jesus that *there is* nothing unclean of itself; but to him who considers any-

14:9 [a]NU-Text omits *and rose.*   14:10 [a]NU-Text reads *of God.*   14:11 [a]Isaiah 45:23

CONSIDER THIS
13:6

THE HIGH CALLING OF GOVERNMENT SERVICE

The largest category of employment in many nations is government. That outrages some citizens, who see government as a massive, wasteful, scandal-plagued bureaucracy. But God takes a different view. If you work in government—as an elected or appointed official, a letter carrier, a police or military officer, a water-meter reader—you'll want to pay special attention to vv. 1–7.

Paul refers to governmental authorities as God's ministers (vv. 4, 6), meaning "servants." It's the same word translated elsewhere as "deacons." The point is, if you work in government, you are ultimately God's worker. Your authority derives not just from the people, but from God Himself. (This is an amazing statement from Paul. He was not living under a democratically elected government, but under an imperial Roman system, probably headed by Nero!)

Government, then, is established by God. That doesn't mean that He approves of everything governments or their representatives do. But good or bad, He chooses to allow them to exist and have authority. He actually works through them to accomplish His purposes.

As a government employee, you are a "minister for

thing to be unclean, to him *it is* unclean. ¹⁵Yet if your brother is grieved because of *your* food, you are no longer walking in love. Do not destroy with your food the one for whom Christ died. ¹⁶Therefore do not let your good be spoken of as evil; ¹⁷for the kingdom of God is not eating and drinking, but righteousness and peace and joy in the Holy Spirit. ¹⁸For he who serves Christ in these things*ᵃ* is acceptable to God and approved by men.

¹⁹Therefore let us pursue the things *which make* for peace and the things by which one may edify another. ²⁰Do not destroy the work of God for the sake of food. All things indeed *are* pure, but *it is* evil for the man who eats with offense. ²¹*It is* good neither to eat meat nor drink wine nor *do anything* by which your brother stumbles or is offended or is made weak.*ᵃ* ²²Do you have faith?*ᵃ* Have *it* to yourself before God. Happy is he who does not condemn himself in what he approves. ²³But he who doubts is condemned if he eats, because *he does* not *eat* from faith; for whatever *is* not from faith is sin.*ᵃ*

(Bible text continued on page 569)

14:18 ᵃNU-Text reads this.   14:21 ᵃNU-Text omits or is offended or is made weak.
14:22 ᵃNU-Text reads The faith which you have—have.   14:23 ᵃM-Text puts Romans 16:25–27 here.

good." In what way? This passage describes one important category of governmental authority—policing citizens by motivating them to pursue good and punishing those who do evil. Of course, your work in the system may involve very different tasks. Still, God wants you to be a "minister for good" by helping society function, by meeting the needs of people, by protecting the rights of people, or by defending your country from attack.

With authority comes responsibility and accountability. As a "minister of God" you will answer to Him for your decisions and actions. If God promises to avenge the evil that citizens commit, how much more will He avenge the evil that those in authority commit? ◆

For a larger perspective on everyday work, see "People at Work," Heb. 2:7.

God gives government the right to revenge, but not private citizens. See "The Morality of Christ," Matt. 5:17–48.

DEBT-FREE LIVING

CONSIDER THIS 13:8 Paul's admonition to owe nothing but love (v. 8) is a powerful reminder of God's distaste for all forms of unpaid debt.

Usually we think of debt in terms of monetary loans. But in light of the context of this passage (13:1–7, 9–10), Paul seems to have a broader view of debt in mind (v. 7). He speaks to us of:

- *Taxes,* levies placed on us by governing authorities, such as income and social security taxes.
- *Customs,* tolls and tariffs arising from trade and business, such as highway tolls, airport landing fees, and import fees.
- *Fear,* the respect we owe to those who enforce the law, such as police officers and military personnel.
- *Honor,* the praise we owe to those in high authority, such as judges and elected officials.

All of us are debtors to God's grace. As He has shown us love, we need to extend love to those around us with whom we live and work—even those who tax and govern us.

MATTERS OF CONSCIENCE

One noticeable difference between Christianity and most other religions is that Christians are not bound by ritualistic rules. Paul discusses two examples here in Romans 14: special days of religious observance (vv. 5–13) and food (vv. 2–4, 14–23). However, the principles he sets forth apply to all matters of conscience, the "gray" areas of life for which Scripture prescribes no specific behavior one way or another.

Special observances and food were apparently trouble spots for the Roman believers. No doubt those from Jewish backgrounds brought their heritage of strict Sabbath-keeping and were shocked to find Gentile believers to whom Sabbath days were inconsequential. Likewise, some from pagan backgrounds may have encouraged the church to form its own counterparts to the festival days they had practiced in their former religions. Either way, the keeping of "holy days" created tension in the church.

So did the issue of eating meat. The pagan religions of the day offered meat as sacrifices to their idols. The meat was then sold to the general public. As it tended to be among the choicest cuts, it made for good eating. But many believers objected to eating such meat, or meat of any kind, lest they give tacit approval to the practice of idolatry. Others, however, saw no problem (v. 2). Again, Christians lined up on both sides of the issue. Predictably, people began to question each other's spirituality and dispute over whose position was "right" (v. 1).

Do these situations sound familiar? Perhaps meat sacrificed to idols is not an issue for believers today. But plenty of issues have managed to divide believers today. Does Paul offer any perspective on settling such disputes? Yes:

(1) No Christian should judge another regarding disputable things (vv. 3–4, 13). We may have opinions about what is right and wrong. But Christ is the Judge, for us and for others.

(2) Each person needs to come to his or her own convictions regarding matters of conscience (vv. 5, 22–23). God has given us a mind and the responsibility to think things through and decide what is best for ourselves in cases where the Scriptures are not clear. Unexamined morality is as irresponsible as no morality.

(3) We are not totally free to do as we please; we must answer to the Lord for our behavior (vv. 7–8, 12).

(4) We should avoid offending others by flaunting our liberty (v. 13). A "stumbling block" is an ancient metaphor for giving offense. It is easy to offend believers whose consciences are immature—that is, who lack the knowledge and confidence of their liberty in Christ (v. 2; 1 Cor. 8:9–12). This can happen in two ways: through trampling on their sensibilities by deliberately engaging in practices they find offensive; or through tempting them to engage in something they regard as sin. Even actions that are not inherently sinful can produce sin if they cause others to stumble.

(5) We should practice love, pursuing peace in the body and that which builds others up in the faith (vv. 15, 19). Christianity is just as concerned with community and healthy relationships as it is with morality. To be sure, there are matters that are worth fighting for. But where God is either silent or has left room for personal choice, believers need to practice tolerance and consider what is best for all. ◆

In a related text, Paul appeals to conscience for settling controversial issues. See "Gray Areas," 1 Cor. 8:1–13.

CHAPTER 15

Show Compassion to All

¹We then who are strong ought to bear with the scruples of the weak, and not to please ourselves. ²Let each of us please *his* neighbor for *his* good, leading to edification. ³For even Christ did not please Himself; but as it is written, "The reproaches of those who reproached You fell on Me."*ᵃ* ⁴For whatever things were written before were written for our learning, that we through the patience and comfort of the Scriptures might have hope. ⁵Now may the God of patience and comfort grant you to be like-minded toward one another, according to Christ Jesus, ⁶that you may with one mind *and* one mouth glorify the God and Father of our Lord Jesus Christ.

15:7–12
see pg. 570

⁷Therefore receive one another, just as Christ also received us,*ᵃ* to the glory of God. ⁸Now I say that Jesus Christ has become a servant to the circumcision for the truth of God, to confirm the promises *made* to the fathers, ⁹and that the Gentiles might glorify God for *His* mercy, as it is written:

"For this reason I will confess to You among the
    Gentiles,
And sing to Your name."*ᵃ*

¹⁰And again he says:

"Rejoice, O Gentiles, with His people!"*ᵃ*

¹¹And again:

"Praise the Lord, all you Gentiles!
Laud Him, all you peoples!"*ᵃ*

¹²And again, Isaiah says:

"There shall be a root of Jesse;
And He who shall rise to reign over the Gentiles,
In Him the Gentiles shall hope."*ᵃ*

¹³Now may the God of hope fill you with all joy and peace in believing, that you may abound in hope by the power of the Holy Spirit.

Paul's Confidence in His Readers

¹⁴Now I myself am confident concerning you, my brethren, that you also are full of goodness, filled with all knowledge, able also to admonish one another.*ᵃ* ¹⁵Nevertheless, brethren, I have written more boldly to you on *some*

15:3 *ᵃ*Psalm 69:9   15:7 *ᵃ*NU-Text and M-Text read *you.*   15:9 *ᵃ*2 Samuel 22:50; Psalm 18:49
15:10 *ᵃ*Deuteronomy 32:43   15:11 *ᵃ*Psalm 117:1   15:12 *ᵃ*Isaiah 11:10   15:14 *ᵃ*M-Text
reads *others.*

ARE SUNDAYS SPECIAL?

CONSIDER THIS
14:5–13

In the Old Testament, God commanded the Hebrews to set aside one day a week as a "sabbath," a holy day of rest (Ex. 20:8–11; Is. 58:13–14; Jer. 17:19–27). Yet here in Romans, Paul seems to take a nondirective posture toward the Sabbath (14:5). Does that mean that there is no such thing as a "Lord's day," that God's people are no longer required to observe a Sabbath, whether it be Saturday or Sunday?

Not exactly. For Paul, *every day* should be lived for the Lord because we are the Lord's possession (v. 8). If we act as if Sunday is the Lord's day but the other six days belong to us, then we've got a major misunderstanding. All seven days of the week belong to the Lord.

So the real question is, should one of those days be observed in a special way, in light of God's instructions regarding a sabbath? Paul says that neither pressure from other people nor tradition should bind our consciences. Instead, we are to seek guidance from the Spirit of God as to what we should do. Having inspired the Scriptures, God will help us determine what we should do as we study them.

For more on God's intentions regarding the Sabbath, see "The Sabbath," Heb. 4:1–13.

GOD'S RAINBOW

CONSIDER THIS *15:7–12* **Societies and their systems tend to encourage people to divide along racial, ethnic, and cultural lines, or else to abandon their distinctives by assimilating into the dominant power group. Paul called for a different approach. He didn't ask Jews to give up their Jewish heritage and become Gentiles, nor did he ask Gentiles to become Jews. Instead, he affirmed the rich ethnic backgrounds of both groups while challenging them to live together in unity (v. 7).**

That kind of unity is costly, and the attempt to practice it is always under attack. Yet that is the church that God calls us to—a diverse body of people who are unified around Christ. Our backgrounds—whether Japanese, Anglo-Saxon, African, Middle Eastern, Puerto Rican, Chinese, Italian, or whatever—are God's gifts to each of us and to the church. He has placed us in our families as He has seen fit. We can rejoice in the background He has given us and be enriched by the background He has given others.

points, as reminding you, because of the grace given to me by God, [16]that I might be a minister of Jesus Christ to the Gentiles, ministering the gospel of God, that the offering of the Gentiles might be acceptable, sanctified by the Holy Spirit. [17]Therefore I have reason to glory in Christ Jesus in the things *which pertain* to God. [18]For I will not dare to speak of any of those things which Christ has not accomplished through me, in word and deed, to make the Gentiles obedient— [19]in mighty signs and wonders, by the power of the Spirit of God, so that from Jerusalem and round about to Illyricum I have fully preached the gospel of Christ. [20]And so I have made it my aim to preach the gospel, not where Christ was named, lest I should build on another man's foundation, [21]but as it is written:

> "To whom He was not announced, they shall see;
> And those who have not heard shall understand."[a]

Paul Expects to Preach the Gospel at Rome

[22]For this reason I also have been much hindered from coming to you. [23]But now no longer having a place in these parts, and having a great desire these many years to come to *15:24* you, [24]whenever I journey to Spain, I shall come to you.[a] For I hope to see you on my journey, and to be helped on my way there by you, if first I may enjoy your *company* for a while. [25]But now I am going to Jerusalem to minister to the saints. [26]For it pleased those from Macedonia and Achaia to make a certain contribution for the poor among the saints who are in Jerusalem. [27]It pleased them indeed, and they are their debtors. For if the Gentiles have been partakers of their spiritual things, their duty is also to minister to them in material things. [28]Therefore, when I have performed this and have sealed to them this fruit, I shall go by way of you to Spain. [29]But I know that when I come to you, I shall come in the fullness of the blessing of the gospel[a] of Christ.

[30]Now I beg you, brethren, through the Lord Jesus Christ,

15:21 [a]Isaiah 52:15   15:24 [a]NU-Text omits I shall come to you (and joins Spain with the next sentence).   15:29 [a]NU-Text omits of the gospel.

Rest Stop in Rome

A CLOSER LOOK *15:24* *Many Bible readers assume that Paul's main goal in his work was to reach Rome, where he would preach the gospel to the leaders of the empire. But he intended to stop at Rome on his way to another strategic target, Spain (v. 24). He probably never made it that far. But why was Spain so important? See "All Roads Lead to Rome—and Beyond," Acts 28:28–31.*

and through the love of the Spirit, that you strive together with me in prayers to God for me, ³¹that I may be delivered from those in Judea who do not believe, and that my service for Jerusalem may be acceptable to the saints, ³²that I may come to you with joy by the will of God, and may be refreshed together with you. ³³Now the God of peace *be* with you all. Amen.

CHAPTER 16

Personal Greetings

16:1

¹I commend to you Phoebe our sister, who is a servant of the church in Cenchrea, ²that you may receive her in the Lord in a manner worthy of the saints, and assist her in whatever business

---

PERSONALITY PROFILE: PRISCILLA AND AQUILA

FOR YOUR INFO 16:3–5

Names mean: "Eagle" (Aquila); "ancient" (Priscilla, who was also called Prisca).

Background: Aquila was originally from Pontus in Asia Minor, bordering the Black Sea. They lived in Rome before Claudius forced all Jews to leave Rome. They then relocated to Corinth, and later to Ephesus. Eventually they returned to Rome.

Family: Priscilla might have grown up in a wealthy Roman family; Aquila might have been a Jewish freedman. Marrying across ethnic and socioeconomic lines was unusual in their day.

Occupation: Tentmaking—the manufacture of affordable mobile buildings for living, working, and traveling.

Best known today for: Taking Apollos the speaker aside and explaining to him the way of God more accurately (Acts 18:26); also helping to start at least three churches—at Rome, Corinth, and Ephesus.

PHOEBE

CONSIDER THIS 16:1

Paul called Phoebe (v. 1) a *diakonos* (translated here as "servant," elsewhere as "deacon" or "minister") of the church at Cenchrea, the eastern port of Corinth. Does that means she held a formal position of responsibility? Possibly. Paul frequently referred to himself as a *diakonos* and used the same term in writing about male coworkers such as Apollos, Tychicus, Epaphras, and Timothy (1 Cor. 3:5; Eph. 6:21; Col. 1:7; 4:7; 1 Thess. 3:2).

Our understanding of exactly what it meant to be a *diakonos* in the early church is incomplete. Where the word appears in secular literature of the first century it refers to a helper of any sort who was not a slave. Whatever the role entailed, Paul commended Phoebe to the believers in Rome as a valued sister and one to be esteemed as one of his coworkers.

One important way that Phoebe may have assisted Paul was by taking his letter to Rome. The terms used to describe her suggest that she was a wealthy businesswoman of some influence. Perhaps she agreed to carry the document with her on business to the capital. Since couriers in the ancient world served as representatives of those who sent them, it is possible that Phoebe not only delivered the letter but also read it at different gatherings of Christians and discussed its contents with them.

JUNIA

CONSIDER THIS 16:7

Paul sends greetings to two fellow countrymen and fellow prisoners, Andronicus and Junia (v. 7). Was Junia a man or a woman? It is impossible to tell from the Greek text. The name could just as well be translated Ju-

(continued on next page)

(continued from previous page)

nias. However, in v. 3 Paul greets a couple, Priscilla and Aquila, then a man, Epaenetus (v. 4) and a woman, Mary (v. 5). Then he comes to Andronicus and Junia, whom he names together. Were they a couple, like Priscilla and Aquila? Again, it is impossible to say with certainty, but it is at least possible.

The interesting thing is that Paul describes these two as "of note among the apostles." That could mean either that they were actually apostles themselves or simply that the apostles held them in high esteem. If the former, and if Junia was a woman, that would mean that the early church had female apostles as well as male, and that it was not a movement led exclusively by men.

Right from the start the apostles were joined by women who had followed Christ. See "An Inclusive Prayer Meeting," Acts 1:14.

she has need of you; for indeed she has been a helper of many and of myself also.

✓ 16:3–5
see pg. 571

³Greet Priscilla and Aquila, my fellow workers in Christ Jesus, ⁴who risked their own necks for my life, to whom not only I give thanks, but also all the churches of the Gentiles. ⁵Likewise *greet* the church that is in their house.

Greet my beloved Epaenetus, who is the firstfruits of Achaia[a] to Christ. ⁶Greet Mary, who labored much for us.

♡ 16:7
see pg. 571

⁷Greet Andronicus and Junia, my countrymen and my fellow prisoners, who are of note among the apostles, who also were in Christ before me.

⁸Greet Amplias, my beloved in the Lord. ⁹Greet Urbanus, our fellow worker in Christ, and Stachys, my beloved. ¹⁰Greet Apelles, approved in Christ. Greet those who are of the *household* of Aristobulus. ¹¹Greet Herodion, my countryman.[a] Greet those who are of the *household* of Narcissus who are in the Lord.

✓ 16:12

✓ 16:13

¹²Greet Tryphena and Tryphosa, who have labored in the Lord. Greet the beloved Persis, who labored much in the Lord. ¹³Greet Rufus, chosen in the Lord,

16:5 ᵃNU-Text reads *Asia.*   16:11 ᵃOr *relative*

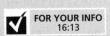

✓ FOR YOUR INFO
16:13

WHO WAS PAUL'S MOTHER?

n greeting Rufus and "his *mother* and mine" (v. 13, italics added), Paul was probably not indicating his own actual mother, but rather a woman who played an important role in Paul's life.

The apostle often used the image of a father or mother to describe his own unique relationship with certain Christians (1 Cor. 4:15; 1 Thess. 2:7), and some believers he called his children (1 Cor. 4:14; 1 Tim. 1:2; 2 Tim. 1:2; 2:1). He never explained exactly what he meant by those terms, but we can assume that those who received his letters knew what he meant. Apparently Paul had been instrumental in their lives in a way that a parent might be with a child.

In a similar way, the woman greeted in Romans 16:13 must have been especially important to Paul. Perhaps she had helped to nurture his faith, somewhat like Priscilla and Aquila with Apollos (see "Marketplace Mentors: Priscilla and Aquila," Acts 18:24–26; and "Apollos," Acts 18:24–28). Or perhaps she had helped to support Paul financially or in prayer. Whatever the case, he felt deeply enough toward her to refer to her as his mother.

Of Paul's actual mother, almost nothing is known. We

and his mother and mine. ¹⁴Greet Asyncritus, Phlegon, Hermas, Patrobas, Hermes, and the brethren who are with them. ¹⁵Greet Philologus and Julia, Nereus and his sister, and Olympas, and all the saints who are with them.

¹⁶Greet one another with a holy kiss. The*a* churches of Christ greet you.

Warnings against False Teachers

¹⁷Now I urge you, brethren, note those who cause divisions and offenses, contrary to the doctrine which you learned, and avoid them. ¹⁸For those who are such do not serve our Lord Jesus*a* Christ, but their own belly, and by smooth words and flattering speech deceive the hearts of the simple. ¹⁹For your obedience has become known to all. Therefore I am glad on your behalf; but I want you to be wise in what is good, and simple concerning evil. ²⁰And the God of peace will crush Satan under your feet shortly.

The grace of our Lord Jesus Christ *be* with you. Amen.

Final Greetings and a Benediction

²¹Timothy, my fellow worker, and Lucius, Jason, and Sosipater, my countrymen, greet you.

²²I, Tertius, who wrote *this* epistle, greet you in the Lord.

16:16 *a*NU-Text reads *All the churches.*   16:18 *a*NU-Text and M-Text omit *Jesus.*

can deduce that she must have been Jewish, because Paul was a Jew, and a Jewish heritage was determined through the mother. Paul said that he was born a Roman citizen (Acts 22:28), which meant his father must have been a Roman citizen before him. Apparently Paul was not their only child, for Luke mentions a sister (Acts 23:16).

However, we do have a clue as to the identity of the woman mentioned in Romans 16. The context implies that she was Rufus' actual mother. Rufus is probably the same man mentioned as one of the sons of Simon, the man who helped carry Jesus' cross (see Mark 15:21). If so, Rufus and his family were from Cyrene on the northern coast of Africa and were well known to the early church.

Whatever role Rufus' mother had in Paul's life, he certainly didn't forget her. Do you remember your mothers and fathers in the faith? ◆

Learn more about Paul's background through the two profiles, "Saul" and "Paul," Acts 13:2–3.

PAUL'S FEMALE COWORKERS

FOR YOUR INFO 16:12 **As Paul traveled throughout the Mediterranean, many believers labored with him to spread the message of Christ. Not a few of these valuable associates were women, several of whom are listed here in Romans 16.**

Paul literally owed his life to some of these coworkers. In several of his letters he lists their names and expresses his gratitude to them. Here are some of the women mentioned:

WOMEN OF THE EARLY CHURCH

Apphia (Philem. 2)
Euodia (Phil. 4:2–3)
Junia (possibly a woman, Rom. 16:7)
Lydia (Acts 16:13–40)
Mary of Rome (Rom. 16:6)
Nympha (Col. 4:15)
Persis (Rom. 16:12)
Phoebe (Rom. 16:1–2)
Priscilla (Acts 18:1–28; Rom. 16:3; 1 Cor. 16:19; 2 Tim. 4:19)
Syntyche (Phil. 4:2–3)
Tryphena (Rom. 16:12)
Tryphosa (Rom. 16:12)

Women also played a major part in Jesus' life and work, and helped take His message to the far reaches of the Roman world. See "The Women around Jesus," John 19:25; and the table, "Women and the Growth of Christianity," Phil. 4:3.

²³Gaius, my host and *the host* of the whole church, greets you. Erastus, the treasurer of the city, greets you, and Quartus, a brother. ²⁴The grace of our Lord Jesus Christ *be* with you all. Amen.ᵃ

²⁵Now to Him who is able to establish you according to my gospel and the preaching of Jesus Christ, according to the revelation of the mystery kept secret since the world began ²⁶but now made manifest, and by the prophetic Scriptures made known to all nations, according to the commandment of the everlasting God, for obedience to the faith— ²⁷to God, alone wise, *be* glory through Jesus Christ forever. Amen.ᵃ

16:24 ᵃNU-Text omits this verse.   16:27 ᵃM-Text puts Romans 16:25–27 after Romans 14:23.

A Collection of Sinners

Have you ever sighed, "I wish my church could be more like the church of the first century"? Perhaps you have in mind a small, closely knit community of believers who are radically committed to each other and, despite their number, are turning the community upside down with the gospel. What an exciting ideal! Unfortunately, the reality of the first churches probably wouldn't match it.

The church at Corinth is a good case in point. It had several excellent teachers and leaders, yet it struggled with the same problems many churches face today. The Corinthian church was an example of what churches look like, made up as they are of sinners saved by grace.

Depending on your expectations, the two Corinthian letters can make for encouraging reading. They point to the fact that there is no instant spirituality. Discipleship is a process. So if you and other believers around you sometimes seem less than Christlike, take heart! The Corinthians have walked this path before you. Despite their shortcomings, they held a special place in the heart of those who knew them best and helped them get started in the faith.

1 and 2 Corinthians

There is no instant spirituality.

Discipleship is a process.

· ·

CONTENTS

ARTICLES

The Power of Foolishness (1 Cor. 1:18)

Nowhere does the gospel appear more foolish than in today's workplace. Yet the irony is that the message of Christ is far more powerful than even the strongest players in the marketplace can imagine.

Workplace Myths (3:9)

A number of distorted views of work have taken on mythical proportions in Western culture, with devastating effect.

The Scandal of Litigating Christians (6:1–11)

Does the Bible categorically rule out litigation between Christians today?

Career Changes (7:17–24)

Paul says to remain in the situations we were in when we came to faith. Yet most people today change careers at least four times in their lives.

Women and Work in the Ancient World (7:32–35)

Learn about the busy lives that first-century women lived, especially in the large cities of the Roman Empire.

Paying Vocational Christian Workers (9:1–23)

How much should pastors, missionaries, and others who work in churches and ministries be paid? Or should they be paid at all?

The Games (9:24–27)

Corinth was home to one of four prestigious athletic festivals of the Greeks at which competitors vied for glory more than for tangible prizes.

Ten Myths about Christianity, Myth #6: People Become Christians through Social Conditioning (15:9–10)

A common notion today is that religious preference is mainly a result of upbringing. Cultural circumstances play a part in people's religious beliefs, but far more is involved than one's background.

Listening In on a Private Conversation

To read 1 & 2 Corinthians is to read someone else's mail. In contrast to Romans, these letters of Paul are very personal, and perhaps for that reason, very enlightening. What we have here are not fancy ideas dressed up in high-sounding words, but straight talk for a church working through everyday problems.

Actually, several letters passed between Paul and the Corinthians, including at least one between 1 & 2 Corinthians (2 Cor. 2:3). As in listening to one side of a telephone conversation, one has to infer what issues and questions made up the correspondence, based on the two letters that survive.

Paul had written a first, unpreserved letter from Ephesus (during his long stay mentioned in Acts 20:31) in which he warned the congregation about mixing with sexually immoral people (1 Cor. 5:9). That was an ever-present danger in Corinth. Most of the believers there had come from pagan backgrounds (12:2), and perhaps some had previously engaged in the idolatrous practices—including ritual prostitution—of the city's dozens of shrines and pagan temples. (The most prominent, the temple of Aphrodite, employed no less than 1,000 temple prostitutes.)

Paul's first letter must have failed to achieve its purpose, because certain problems persisted (1:11; 16:17). Apparently the Corinthians wrote a letter back to Paul, perhaps to justify their behavior, but also to ask him about other matters. He then wrote 1 Corinthians and minced no words in condemning the congregation's divisions and their continued tolerance of immorality. He also addressed their other concerns, as the repeated use of the words, "Now concerning," indicates (7:1, 25; 8:1; 12:1; 16:1).

But for all its stern language, 1 Corinthians also failed to correct the abuses. So Paul paid a visit to the church, but he was rebuffed (2 Cor. 2:1). Upon his return to Ephesus, he penned an extremely strident letter calculated to shock the stubborn Corinthians into obedience to Christ. (Most scholars believe that that letter has been lost. But some posit that it has been preserved in 2 Corinthians as chapters 10–13.)

Paul sent Titus to deliver the bombshell and then waited to hear the outcome. But Titus delayed in returning. As time passed, Paul felt increasingly alarmed that perhaps he had charged the epistle with a bit too much explosive. When he could contain his anxiety no longer, he set out for Corinth by way of Macedonia. But en route he encountered Titus, who, to his relief and joy, reported that the church had at last responded obediently. Heartened by this news, Paul wrote 2 Corinthians to bring healing to the relationship.

Christians today can profit by reading 1 and 2 Corinthians because they get behind the stereotyped images of what the church and the ministry are "supposed" to be. First Corinthians shows that churches are made up of real people living in the real world struggling with real problems. Likewise, 2 Corinthians shows that people in "full-time ministry" struggle with the same problems, doubts, and feelings as anyone else. As we read this correspondence, we need to ask, *If Paul came to my church and my community, what issues and problems would he see? And what would he say?*

• •

Corinth

Beauty mingled with debauchery at Corinth. A "planned" city, it was less than 100 years old at the time of Paul. Stately gates at each city entrance opened onto well-maintained avenues with dozens of buildings and monuments built by the Roman emperors. City walls were lined with picturesque colonnades and countless residential shops. But Corinth was known less for its impressive architecture than its encouragement of gross immorality. See "Corinth" at the Introduction to 2 Corinthians.

THE POWER OF FOOLISHNESS

CONSIDER THIS 1:18 Paul recognized that the gospel appears foolish to most people (v. 18). Nowhere is that more apparent than in the workplace. In a tough, secular business environment, the message of Christ seems wholly out of place. Try to introduce it as relevant and you'll usually find stares of incredulity, if not outright protests.

The irony is that the gospel is far more powerful than even the strongest players in the marketplace can imagine. But it remains impossible to receive except as the Holy Spirit opens a person's eyes.

This has a tremendous bearing on our witness as believers in the workplace. We need to keep communicating the message as persuasively and persistently as we can, all the while asking the Spirit to work His power, both in our own lives and in the lives of those around us.

One thing is certain about evangelism: both non-Christians and Christians feel uncomfortable with it. Fortunately, both have someone to help them in the process. See "Whose Job Is Evangelism?" John 16:8.

The message of the cross may be foolishness, but it was powerful enough to turn the Roman world upside down. See "Power," Acts 1:8.

CHAPTER 1

A Word of Greeting

¹Paul, called *to be* an apostle of Jesus Christ through the will of God, and Sosthenes *our* brother,

²To the church of God which is at Corinth, to those who are sanctified in Christ Jesus, called *to be* saints, with all who in every place call on the name of Jesus Christ our Lord, both theirs and ours:

³Grace to you and peace from God our Father and the Lord Jesus Christ.

⁴I thank my God always concerning you for the grace of God which was given to you by Christ Jesus, ⁵that you were enriched in everything by Him in all utterance and all knowledge, ⁶even as the testimony of Christ was confirmed in you, ⁷so that you come short in no gift, eagerly waiting for the revelation of our Lord Jesus Christ, ⁸who will also confirm you to the end, *that you may be* blameless in the day of our Lord Jesus Christ. ⁹God *is* faithful, by whom you were called into the fellowship of His Son, Jesus Christ our Lord.

The Corinthians Are Divided

¹⁰Now I plead with you, brethren, by the name of our Lord Jesus Christ, that you all speak the same thing, and *that* there be no divisions among you, but *that* you be perfectly joined together in the same mind and in the same judgment. ¹¹For it has been declared to me concerning you, my brethren, by those of Chloe's *household,* that there are

1:12 contentions among you. ¹²Now I say this, that each of you says, "I am of Paul," or "I am of Apollos," or "I am of Cephas," or "I am of Christ." ¹³Is Christ divided? Was Paul crucified for you? Or were you baptized in the name of Paul?

¹⁴I thank God that I baptized none of you except Crispus and Gaius, ¹⁵lest anyone should say that I had baptized in my own name. ¹⁶Yes, I also baptized the household of Stephanas. Besides, I do not know whether I baptized any other. ¹⁷For Christ did not send me to baptize, but to preach the gospel, not with wisdom of words, lest the cross of Christ should be made of no effect.

• •

Apollos

A CLOSER LOOK 1:12 *The name Apollos means "destroyer," but Apollos probably wouldn't have wanted the destructive factions that afflicted the church at Corinth. See "Apollos" at Acts 18:24–28.*

Wisdom Is Misunderstood

1:18 ¹⁸For the message of the cross is foolishness to those who are perishing, but to us who are being saved it is the power of God. ¹⁹For it is written:

"I will destroy the wisdom of the wise,
And bring to nothing the understanding of the prudent."ᵃ

²⁰Where *is* the wise? Where *is* the scribe? Where *is* the disputer of this age? Has not God made foolish the wisdom of this world? ²¹For since, in the wisdom of God, the world through wisdom did not know God, it pleased God through the foolishness of the message preached to save those who believe. ²²For Jews request a sign, and Greeks seek after wisdom; **1:23** ²³but we preach Christ crucified, to the Jews a stumbling block and to the Greeksᵃ foolishness, ²⁴but to those who are called, both Jews and Greeks, Christ the power of God and the wisdom of God. ²⁵Because the foolishness of God is wiser than men, and the weakness of God is stronger than men.

1:26 see pg. 580 ²⁶For you see your calling, brethren, that not many wise according to the flesh, not many mighty, not many noble, *are called.* ²⁷But God has chosen the foolish things of the world to put to shame the wise, and God has chosen the weak things of the world to put to shame the things which are mighty; ²⁸and the base things of the world and the things which are despised God has chosen, and the things which are not, to bring to nothing the things that are, ²⁹that no flesh should glory in His presence. ³⁰But of Him you are in Christ Jesus, who became for us wisdom from God—and righteousness and sanctification and redemption— ³¹that, as it is written, "He who glories, let him glory in the LORD."ᵃ

CHAPTER 2

Paul's Initial Visit Was in Weakness

¹And I, brethren, when I came to you, did not come with excellence of speech or of wisdom declaring to you the testimonyᵃ of God. ²For I determined not to know anything among you except Jesus Christ and Him crucified. ³I was with you in weakness, in fear, and in much trembling. ⁴And my speech and my preaching *were* not with persuasive words of humanᵃ wisdom, but in demonstration of the

(Bible text continued on page 581)

1:19 ᵃIsaiah 29:14   *1:23* ᵃNU-Text reads *Gentiles.*   *1:31* ᵃJeremiah 9:24   *2:1* ᵃNU-Text reads *mystery.*   *2:4* ᵃNU-Text omits *human.*

QUOTE UNQUOTE

CONSIDER THIS 1:23 *Paul's message was "Christ crucified" (v. 23). The gospel has not changed, and the same bold message is needed today:*

I simply argue that the cross be raised again at the center of the marketplace, as well as on the steeple of the church. I am recovering the claim that Jesus was not crucified between two candles, but on a cross between two thieves; on the town garbage heap; at a crossroad so cosmopolitan that they had to write his title in Latin and Greek . . . at the kind of place where cynics talk smut, and thieves curse, and soldiers gamble. Because that's where He died. And that is what He died about. And that is where churchmen ought to be and what churchmen should be about.

George MacLeod, Founder of the Scottish IONA Community, recipient of the Templeton Award for religious leadership

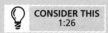
MYTH #5

10 MYTHS ABOUT CHRISTIANITY

MYTH: CHRISTIANITY IS JUST A CRUTCH FOR THE WEAK

Many people today accept a number of myths about Christianity, with the result that they never respond to Jesus as He really is. This is one of ten articles that speak to some of those misconceptions. For a list of all ten, see 1 Tim. 1:3–4.

The believers at Corinth tended to think more highly of themselves than they ought to have. The result was conflict and division in the church. So Paul pointed out that most of them had little of which to boast (v. 26; see also 6:9–11). On the whole they were weak, sinful people saved only by the grace of God.

Today, the grace of God still reaches out to the weak, the downcast, the broken, and the oppressed. Perhaps for that reason, people who pride themselves on their strength and self-sufficiency have little use for the gospel. Indeed, some despise a faith that resists the proud but promises hope to the humble.

Is Christianity just another crutch for people who can't make it on their own? In one sense, yes. "Those who are well have no need of a physician," Jesus said, "but those who are sick. I have not come to call the righteous, but sinners, to repentance" (Luke 5:31–32). Jesus bypasses those who pretend to be invincible, those who think they have it all together. Instead He reaches out to those who know that something is wrong, that their lives are "sick" with "illnesses" such as greed, lust,

cruelty, and selfishness.

Jesus knows that no one is spiritually healthy. No one is righteous enough to stand before a holy God. That's why He came into this world, to restore people to God. The good news is that Christ gives us the power to overcome sin and the ways it pulls us down time after time.

What happens to the "weak" who avail themselves of this "crutch"? Consider Mother Teresa, who emerged from an insignificant nunnery to love the helpless and homeless of Calcutta and became a worldwide symbol of compassion. Or consider Alexander Solzhenitsyn, a forgotten political prisoner rotting away in the gulag system of Stalinist Russia. Surrendering himself to Jesus, he gained renewed strength to challenge a totalitarian regime on behalf of human dignity and freedom.

These are but two examples from the millions who have thrown away the self-styled crutches on which they used to limp along the road of life, opting instead for the seasoned wood of the cross of Christ which has transformed their weakness into strength.

In one sense, Christianity is a crutch for the weak. But those who dismiss it for that reason usually do so to deny their own inadequacies. They use that excuse as a way to evade the claims God has on their lives. They cannot accept that He takes wounded, fractured people and makes them whole. ◆

Spirit and of power, [5]that your faith should not be in the wisdom of men but in the power of God.

The Message Was God's Wisdom

[6]However, we speak wisdom among those who are mature, yet not the wisdom of this age, nor of the rulers of this age, who are coming to nothing. [7]But we speak the wisdom of God in a mystery, the hidden *wisdom* which God ordained before the ages for our glory, [8]which none of the rulers of this age knew; for had they known, they would not have crucified the Lord of glory.

[9]But as it is written:

"Eye has not seen, nor ear heard,
Nor have entered into the heart of man
The things which God has prepared for those who love Him."[a]

[10]But God has revealed *them* to us through His Spirit. For the Spirit searches all things, yes, the deep things of God. [11]For what man knows the things of a man except the spirit of the man which is in him? Even so no one knows the things of God except the Spirit of God. [12]Now we have received, not the spirit of the world, but the Spirit who is from God, that we might know the things that have been freely given to us by God.

[13]These things we also speak, not in words which man's wisdom teaches but which the Holy[a] Spirit teaches, comparing spiritual things with spiritual. [14]But the natural man does not receive the things of the Spirit of God, for they are foolishness to him; nor can he know *them,* because they are spiritually discerned. [15]But he who is spiritual judges all things, yet he himself is *rightly* judged by no one. [16]For "who has known the mind of the LORD that he may instruct Him?"[a] But we have the mind of Christ.

CHAPTER 3

The Apostle's Role Misunderstood

[1]And I, brethren, could not speak to you as to spiritual *people* but as to carnal, as to babes in Christ. [2]I fed you with milk and not with solid food; for until now you were not able *to receive it,* and even now you are still not able; [3]for you are still carnal. For where *there are* envy, strife, and divisions among you, are you not carnal and behaving like *mere* men? [4]For when one says, "I am of Paul," and another, "I am of Apollos," are you not carnal?

2:9 [a]Isaiah 64:4   2:13 [a]NU-Text omits *Holy.*   2:16 [a]Isaiah 40:13

ARE WE TO JUDGE ALL THINGS?

CONSIDER THIS 2:15 Paul's claim about judging all things (v. 15) sounds rather presumptuous. Is he urging believers to become moral policemen, passing judgment on everyone and everything around us?

Yes and no. Paul was challenging the spiritually immature believers at Corinth to grow up by applying spiritual discernment to the world around them. In this passage he mentions three categories of people:

- *natural* (v. 14), those without Christ, still living in the lost condition in which they were born;
- *spiritual* (v. 15), believers in Christ who have been born of the Spirit and in whom the Spirit of God lives and is producing growth; and
- *carnal* (3:1), believers who remain immature in the faith because they don't allow the Spirit to work in their lives.

Spiritual people "judge" all things that come their way (v. 15) in the sense of scrutinizing, examining, and investigating spiritual value and implications. This is not something that we should do merely as individuals, but also corporately with other believers. For example, in the workplace Christians in various occupations need to band together to explore how the faith applies to particular vocations. By analyzing work situations in light of Scripture, we can discern what the issues are and how we might respond with Christlikeness.

"Judging all things" has nothing to do with damning others, but with recognizing and doing what God would want. Instead of pride, it calls for humility, since God will be the final Judge of everything we do (2 Cor. 5:10).

WHO GETS THE CREDIT?

CONSIDER THIS **3:5–8** Paul pointed out that the work of planting the church at Corinth was a joint venture between himself, Apollos, and the Lord (vv. 5–8). Actually, many others were involved as well. But the point was that cooperation, not competition, is what God desires.

Paul was speaking about the start-up of a church, but the principles apply in the workplace as well. An attitude of competition worries about who gets the credit for success, which is really a selfish concern. By contrast, cooperative efforts over time generally result in achievements far greater than what any individual could do in isolation. That's because the skill, insight, and energy in an organization's work force have enormous potential. But that potential will never be realized if everyone's chief objective is to take credit for results.

Who gets the credit where you work? Do you promote cooperation toward mutual goals rather than competition between individual agendas?

• • • • • • • • • • • • • • • •

Apollos was a silver-tongued orator, but he learned much of his theology from a hard-working couple. See his profile, Acts 18:24–28.

THE ULTIMATE PERFORMANCE REVIEW

CONSIDER THIS **3:13–15** People often joke about standing before God and having their lives examined. But the picture Paul paints in vv. 9–15 is anything but funny. He is dead serious about a day of accountability for believers. Most of us are familiar with performance reviews on

(continued on next page)

3:5–8 [5]Who then is Paul, and who is Apollos, but ministers through whom you believed, as the Lord gave to each one? [6]I planted, Apollos watered, but God gave the increase. [7]So then neither he who plants is anything, nor he who waters, but God who gives the increase. [8]Now he who plants and he who waters are one, and each one will receive his own reward according to his own labor.

A New Building for God

3:9 **see pg. 584** [9]For we are God's fellow workers; you are God's field, *you are* God's building. [10]According to the grace of God which was given to me, as a wise master builder I have laid the foundation, and another builds on it. But let each one take heed how he builds on it. [11]For no other foundation can anyone lay than that which is laid, which is Jesus Christ. [12]Now if anyone builds on this foundation *with* gold, silver, precious stones, wood, hay, straw, **3:13–15** [13]each one's work will become clear; for the Day will declare it, because it will be revealed by fire; and the fire will test each one's work, of what sort it is. [14]If anyone's work which he has built on *it* endures, he will receive a reward. [15]If anyone's work is burned, he will suffer loss; but he himself will be saved, yet so as through fire.

[16]Do you not know that you are the temple of God and *that* the Spirit of God dwells in you? [17]If anyone defiles the temple of God, God will destroy him. For the temple of God is holy, which *temple* you are.

[18]Let no one deceive himself. If anyone among you seems to be wise in this age, let him become a fool that he may become wise. [19]For the wisdom of this world is foolishness with God. For it is written, "He catches the wise in their own craftiness";[a] [20]and again, "The LORD knows the thoughts of the wise, that they are futile."[a] [21]Therefore let no one boast in men. For all things are yours: [22]whether Paul or Apollos or Cephas, or the world or life or death, or things present or things to come—all are yours. [23]And you *are* Christ's, and Christ *is* God's.

CHAPTER 4

No Room for Boasting

[1]Let a man so consider us, as servants of Christ and stewards of the mysteries of God. [2]Moreover it is required in stewards that one be found faithful. [3]But **4:3–5** **see pg. 586** with me it is a very small thing that I

3:19 [a]Job 5:13   3:20 [a]Psalm 94:11

should be judged by you or by a human court.*a* In fact, I do not even judge myself. 4For I know of nothing against myself, yet I am not justified by this; but He who judges me is the Lord. 5Therefore judge nothing before the time, until the Lord comes, who will both bring to light the hidden things of darkness and reveal the counsels of the hearts. Then each one's praise will come from God.

6Now these things, brethren, I have figuratively transferred to myself and Apollos for your sakes, that you may learn in us not to think beyond what is written, that none of you may be puffed up on behalf of one against the other. 7For who makes you differ *from another?* And what do you have that you did not receive? Now if you did indeed receive *it,* why do you boast as if you had not received *it?*

Fools for Christ

8You are already full! You are already rich! You have reigned as kings without us—and indeed I could wish you did reign, that we also might reign with you! 9For I think that God has displayed us, the apostles, last, as men condemned to death; for we have been made a spectacle to the world, both to angels and to men. 10We *are* fools for Christ's sake, but you *are* wise in Christ! We *are* weak, but you *are* strong! You *are* distinguished, but we *are* dishonored! 11To the present hour we both hunger and thirst, and we are poorly clothed, and beaten, and homeless. 12And we labor, working with our own hands. Being reviled, we bless; being persecuted, we endure; 13being defamed, we entreat. We have been made as the filth of the world, the offscouring of all things until now.

Paul's Care for the Corinthians

14I do not write these things to shame you, but as my beloved children I warn *you.* 15For though you might have ten thousand instructors in Christ, yet *you do* not *have* many fathers; for in Christ Jesus I have begotten you through the gospel. 16Therefore I urge you, imitate me. 17For this reason I have sent Timothy to you, who is my beloved and faithful son in the Lord, who will remind you of my ways in Christ, as I teach everywhere in every church.

18Now some are puffed up, as though I were not coming to you. 19But I will come to you shortly, if the Lord wills, and I will know, not the word of those who are puffed up, but the power. 20For the kingdom of God *is* not in word but in power. 21What do you want? Shall I come to you with a rod, or in love and a spirit of gentleness?

(Bible text continued on page 586)

4:3 *a*Literally *day*

(continued from previous page)

the job. Paul describes the ultimate performance review—the moment when we stand before God and He evaluates the worth of our lives on the earth, not for salvation but for reward or loss.

Paul uses the image of metal being purified in a refining fire (vv. 13–15). The fire burns away the worthless impurities, leaving only what is valuable. Based on the values set forth in many passages of Scripture, we can imagine the kinds of things that constitute "gold, silver, [and] precious stones": acts of charity and kindness; ethical decision-making; the pursuit of justice and fair play; keeping our word; courage and perseverance in the face of opposition and persecution; humility; communicating the message of Christ to coworkers; honoring our marriage vows; working diligently at the work God gives us; trusting God to keep His promises. Whatever is left when the fire burns down, Paul says, God will reward us for it (v. 14).

Conversely, we can envision what sorts of "wood, hay, [and] straw" will burn up: the lies we've told; ways we may have cheated customers; abuse heaped on family and relatives; manipulation of situations to our advantage; selfishness of all kinds; the squandering of income on trivial luxuries; turning a deaf ear to the poor; damage allowed to our environment; the systems created to lock ourselves into power and lock others out; the arrogance of self-sufficiency; lack of faith.

When the smoke clears, what will be left of your life?

WORKPLACE MYTHS

Paul called himself one of God's "fellow workers" (v. 9). In a similar way, every one of us is a coworker with God (see "People at Work," Heb. 2:7). Yet certain distorted views of work have taken on mythical proportions in Western culture. They've had devastating effect on both the people and the message of Christ. Here's a sampling of these pernicious myths, along with a few points of rebuttal:

Myth: Church work is the only work that has any real spiritual value.

In other words, everyday work in the "secular" world counts for nothing of lasting value. Only "sacred" work matters to God.

Fact: Christianity makes no distinction between the "sacred" and the "secular."

All of life is to be lived under Christ's lordship. So when it comes to work, all work has essential value to God, and workers will answer to Him for how they have carried out the work He has given to them (1 Cor. 3:13).

Myth: The heroes of the faith are ministers and missionaries. "Lay" workers remain second-class.

This follows from the previous idea. If "sacred" work is the only work with eternal value, then "sacred workers" (clergy) are the most valuable workers. The best that "laypeople" can do is to support the clergy and engage in "ministry" during their spare hours.

Fact: God has delegated His work to everybody, not just clergy.

Among the main characters of Scripture are ranchers, farmers, fishermen, vintners, ironworkers, carpenters, tentmakers, textile manufacturers, public officials, construction supervisors and workers, military personnel, financiers, physicians, judges, tax collectors, musicians, sculptors, dancers, poets, and writers, among others. Nowhere does God view these people or their work as "second class" or "secular." Rather, their work accomplishes God's work in the world. As we do our work each day, we reflect the very image of God, who is a working God (see "God: The Original Worker," John 5:17). He spent six days working on the creation (Gen. 1:31—2:3), so we merely follow God's example when we work five or six days out of the week.

Myth: Work is a part of the curse.

According to this belief, God punished Adam and Eve for their sin by laying the burden of work on them: "In the sweat of your face you shall eat bread till you return to the ground" (Gen. 3:19). That's why work is so often drudgery, and why the workplace is driven by greed and selfishness.

Fact: Work is a gift from God.

The Bible never calls work a curse, but rather a gift from God (Eccl. 3:13; 5:18–19). God gave Adam and Eve work to do long before they ever sinned (Gen. 2:15), and He commends and commands work long after the fall (Gen. 9:1–7; Col. 3:23; 1 Thess. 4:11; see "Is Work a Curse?" Rom. 8:20–22).

Myth: God is no longer involved in His creation.

For many, if not most, modern-day workers, God is irrelevant in the workplace. He may exist, but He has little to do with everyday matters of the work world. These people don't care much about what God does, and they assume He doesn't care much about what they do, either.

Fact: God remains intimately connected with both His world and its workers.

Scripture knows nothing of a detached Creator. He actively holds the creation together (Col. 1:16–17) and works toward its ultimate restoration from sin (John 5:17; Rom. 8:18–25). He uses the work of people to accomplish many of His purposes. Indeed, believers ultimately work for Christ as their Boss (see "Who's the Boss?" Col. 3:22–24). He takes an active interest in how they do their work (Titus 2:9–10).

Myth: You only go around once in life—so you better make the most of it!

This is the "heaven can wait" perspective. Here-and-now is what matters; it's where the excitement is. Heaven is just a make-believe world of gold-paved streets and never-ending choirs. Boring! Why not enjoy your reward right now? Go for it!

Fact: God is saving the greatest rewards for eternity—and work will be among them.

Scripture doesn't offer much detail about life after death, but it does promise a future society remade by God where work goes on—without the sweat, toil, pain, or futility of the curse (Is. 65:17–25; Rev. 22:2–5). And as for the question of rewards, God plans to hand out rewards for how believers have spent their lives—including their work (1 Cor. 3:9–15).

Myth: The most important day of the week is Friday.

"Thank God it's Friday!" the secular work ethic cries. Because work is drudgery, weekends are for escaping—and catching up. There's no idea of a Sabbath, just a couple of days of respite from the grinding routine.

Fact: God wants us to pursue cycles of meaningful work and restorative rest.

A biblical view of work places a high value on rest. God never intended us to work seven days a week. He still invites us to join Him in a day of rest, renewal, and celebration. That restores us to go back to our work with a sense of purpose and mission. "Thank God it's Monday!" we can begin to say. ◆

AVOIDING MORBID INTROSPECTION

CONSIDER THIS 4:3–5 Paul wisely recognized that even our most conscientious attempts to maintain pure motives fall far short (vv. 3–5). Indwelling sin taints everything we do. But Paul didn't allow that to discourage him from aiming at high motives. Neither did he despair of doing anything good. He was content to do his best in life and let God be his Judge.

Are you free from the chronic worry that your motives are not always pristine? Are you living under the grace of God?

. . . .

Paul knew that someday he would face the ultimate performance review, when God would evaluate both his motives and actions. See 1 Cor. 3:9–15.

COVER-UPS DECEIVE EVERYBODY

CONSIDER THIS 5:1–13 Evil can never be remedied by ignoring or hiding it. In fact, covering it up is the worst that can happen, for like yeast, evil does its terrible work from within (vv. 6–8).

The same is true of believers who live in consistent disobedience to God's expressed will. Their behavior will badly infect the larger groups of which they are a part. It can even lead to a distorted perception of sin in which the group tolerates or even approves of disobedience among its own members yet condemns outsiders for the very same activity (Rom. 1:32; 1 Cor. 5:9–10).

(continued on next page)

CHAPTER 5

Immorality Must Be Dealt With

5:1–13 [1]It is actually reported *that there is* sexual immorality among you, and such sexual immorality as is not even named[a] among the Gentiles—that a man has his father's wife! [2]And you are puffed up, and have not rather mourned, that he who has done this deed might be taken away from among you. [3]For I indeed, as absent in body but present in spirit, have already judged (as though I were present) him who has so done this deed. [4]In the name of our Lord Jesus Christ, when you are gathered together, along with my spirit, with the power of our Lord Jesus Christ, [5]deliver such a one to Satan for the destruction of the flesh, that his spirit may be saved in the day of the Lord Jesus.[a]

[6]Your glorying *is* not good. Do you not know that a little leaven leavens the whole lump? [7]Therefore purge out the old leaven, that you may be a new lump, since you truly are unleavened. For indeed Christ, our Passover, was sacrificed for us.[a] [8]Therefore let us keep the feast, not with old leaven, nor with the leaven of malice and wickedness, but with the unleavened *bread* of sincerity and truth.

[9]I wrote to you in my epistle not to keep company with sexually immoral people. [10]Yet *I certainly did* not *mean* with the sexually immoral people of this world, or with the covetous, or extortioners, or idolaters, since then you would need to go out of the world. [11]But now I have written to you not to keep company with anyone named a brother, who is sexually immoral, or covetous, or an idolater, or a reviler, or a drunkard, or an extortioner—not even to eat with such a person.

[12]For what *have* I *to do* with judging those also who are outside? Do you not judge those who are inside? [13]But those who are outside God judges. Therefore "put away from yourselves the evil person."[a]

CHAPTER 6

Lawsuits before Unbelievers

6:1–11 [1]Dare any of you, having a matter against another, go to law before the unrighteous, and not before the saints? [2]Do you not know that the saints will judge the world? And if the world will be

5:1 [a]NU-Text omits named.   5:5 [a]NU-Text omits Jesus.   5:7 [a]NU-Text omits for us.
5:13 [a]Deuteronomy 17:7; 19:19; 22:21, 24; 24:7

judged by you, are you unworthy to judge the smallest matters? ³Do you not know that we shall judge angels? How much more, things that pertain to this life? ⁴If then you have judgments concerning things pertaining to this life, do you appoint those who are least esteemed by the church to judge? ⁵I say this to your shame. Is it so, that there is not a wise man among you, not even one, who will be able to judge between his brethren? ⁶But brother goes to law against brother, and that before unbelievers!

⁷Now therefore, it is already an utter failure for you that you go to law against one another. Why do you not rather accept wrong? Why do you not rather *let yourselves* be cheated? ⁸No, you yourselves do wrong and cheat, and *you do* these things *to your* brethren! ⁹Do you not know that the unrighteous will not inherit the kingdom of God? Do not be deceived. Neither fornicators, nor idolaters, nor adulterers, nor homosexuals,*ᵃ* nor sodomites, ¹⁰nor thieves, nor covetous, nor drunkards, nor revilers, nor extortioners will inherit the kingdom of God. ¹¹And such were some of you. But you were washed, but you were sanctified, but you were justified in the name of the Lord Jesus and by the Spirit of our God.

Liberty Does Not Mean License

6:12
see pg. 589

¹²All things are lawful for me, but all things are not helpful. All things are lawful for me, but I will not be brought under the power of any. ¹³Foods for the stomach and the stomach for foods, but God will destroy both it and them. Now the body *is* not for sexual immorality but for the Lord, and the Lord for the body. ¹⁴And God both raised up the Lord and will also raise us up by His power.

¹⁵Do you not know that your bodies are members of Christ? Shall I then take the members of Christ and make *them* members of a harlot? Certainly not! ¹⁶Or do you not know that he who is joined to a harlot is one body *with her?* For "the two," He says, "shall become one flesh."*ᵃ* ¹⁷But he who is joined to the Lord is one spirit *with Him.*

¹⁸Flee sexual immorality. Every sin that a man does is outside the body, but he who commits sexual immorality sins against his own body. ¹⁹Or do you not know that your body is the temple of the Holy Spirit *who is* in you, whom you have from God, and you are not your own? ²⁰For you were bought at a price; therefore glorify God in your body*ᵃ* and in your spirit, which are God's.

6:9 *ᵃThat is, catamites* 6:16 *ᵃGenesis 2:24* 6:20 *ᵃNU-Text ends the verse at* body.

(continued from previous page)

Paul challenged the Corinthians to confront the subtle deterioration they had allowed within their congregation (1 Cor. 5:5). However, once the perpetrator had repented, they were then to seek his restoration. Even though corrective activity among believers may be severe, confrontation should always be to promote healing rather than to expel wrongdoers (compare Matt. 18:15–22; 2 Cor. 10:8). There are no throwaway people in the kingdom of God.

THE SCANDAL OF LITIGATING CHRISTIANS

CONSIDER THIS
6:1–11

Scripture is explicit: for a Christian to take another Christian to court is "an utter failure" (v. 7). What, then, should we as believers do when we have disputes that normally call for litigation? Paul recommends that we take the matter before wise believers who can make a judgment (vv. 4–5). But suppose we can't arrange that? Then Paul says it would be better to "accept wrong" than to go before unbelievers for judgment.

Does that categorically rule out lawsuits between Christians today? Not necessarily. Modern Christians disagree over how to apply this passage. Our society is very different from the first-century Roman Empire. But we know that early churches took Paul's instructions literally. They forbade their members to resort to the pagan courts of the day. Instead, they appointed their own elders to judge civil disputes between members.

Those courts gained such a reputation for justice that they even attracted non-Christians, who found them preferable to the notoriously corrupt imperial courts. Eventually, church courts replaced secular courts

(continued on next page)

(continued from previous page)

and for some six centuries were the most important, if not the only, courts in Europe.

Some Christians today are trying to restore this judicial function of the church. In the United States, Christian attorneys are working with church leaders to arbitrate church members' disputes. The decisions can even be legally binding if the disputants agree to that in advance.

How do you settle legal problems when other believers are involved? Are you willing to try everything short of litigation *first,* before even considering going to court?

CHAPTER 7

Instructions to Married Believers

7:1 ¹Now concerning the things of which you wrote to me:

It is good for a man not to touch a woman. ²Nevertheless, because of sexual immorality, let each man have his own

7:3–6
see pg. 590

wife, and let each woman have her own husband. ³Let the husband render to his wife the affection due her, and likewise also the wife to her husband. ⁴The wife does not have authority over her own body, but the husband *does.* And likewise the husband does not have authority over his own body, but the wife *does.* ⁵Do not deprive one another except with consent for a time, that you may give yourselves to fasting and prayer; and come together again so that Satan does not tempt you because of your lack of self-control. ⁶But I say this as a conces-

CONSIDER THIS
7:1

PRACTICAL LESSONS ON MARRIAGE

Have you ever listened in on half of a telephone conversation, trying to figure out what the whole conversation is about? That's what we have in 1 Corinthians 7— half of a very important conversation on marriage between Paul and the Corinthian believers. But we can glean many practical lessons from this passage, for marriage was undergoing profound changes then just as it is today.

Some of the believers in the early church had married before they became Christians. They wondered whether they should divorce their unbelieving spouses in order to remarry Christians and live more wholeheartedly for Christ.

An argument could be made for that. After all, if people's primary loyalty were now to Jesus, shouldn't that invalidate their pre-conversion marriage vows? (Of course, it would also provide them with a convenient excuse to escape bad marriages.)

But Paul didn't recommend that. He viewed the abandonment of one's family as a very serious matter (vv. 10–11), arguing that the believer should stay in the marriage as long as possible (vv. 12–13). However, God desires peace in relationships (v. 15), and that may not be possible in a family where Christian values are not shared. If the unbeliever wants to leave, he or she should be allowed to do so (v. 15).

Many churches in different cultures around the world today are faced with very similar circumstances. For example:

sion, not as a commandment. [7]For I wish that all men were even as I myself. But each one has his own gift from God, one in this manner and another in that.

Instructions to Single Believers

[8]But I say to the unmarried and to the widows: It is good for them if they remain even as I am; [9]but if they cannot exercise self-control, let them marry. For it is better to marry than to burn *with passion.*

Instructions to Those Married to Unbelievers

[10]Now to the married I command, *yet* not I but the Lord: A wife is not to depart from *her* husband. [11]But even if she does depart, let her remain unmarried or be reconciled to *her* husband. And a husband is not to divorce *his* wife.

[12]But to the rest I, not the Lord, say: If any brother has a wife who does not believe, and she is willing to live with him, let him not divorce her. [13]And a woman who has a

❖ ❖ ❖ ❖ ❖ ❖ ❖ ❖ ❖ ❖ ❖ ❖ ❖ ❖ ❖ ❖

- *the new believer who wonders what to do, since her husband isn't interested in church or religion.*
- *the inner-city congregation that has members who live in common-law marriages. What should the church tell them?*
- *the recent immigrant who tells his pastor that he has two families, one in each of two countries. "Should I get rid of one or both of those families?" he wonders.*
- *a tribal chief who wants to join the church—along with his five wives. What should he do with the wives? Divorce them all? Keep one? If so, which one?*

Paul offers no simple solutions for any of these situations, but he does share one piece of very good news: it is possible for one believer to "sanctify" a family, that is, to be an agent of God's love and grace, and perhaps to eventually bring other family members into the faith. No matter how unconventional the situation might be, Scripture doesn't counsel sudden changes. God may have work left to do in that family, and He may use the believer to do it—if he or she stays. ◆

WHAT CONTROLS YOU?

CONSIDER THIS 6:12 **As Christians we live under grace, not law. We enjoy a certain freedom of choice and commitment. But Paul reminds us that our choices and commitments, while freely made, do not always bring freedom (v. 12). Often they overpower us: we no longer possess our possessions—they possess us! We can be consumed by our jobs, our wealth, our houses, our hobbies, even our churches.**

Are there any ways to manage this problem? Here are a few suggestions:

(1) Determine your limits. What can you actually handle? What is realistic?

(2) Let time go by before making decisions and commitments. Sooner or later you need to decide, but very few choices are better made sooner than later.

(3) Pay attention to agreement or disagreement with your spouse and/or a close friend or associate. There is wisdom in mutual decision-making.

(4) To manage the commitment you are taking on, what are you willing to give up? Taking on new responsibilities means trading one set of problems for another. Are you prepared for that?

(5) Commit to giving away as well as taking on. That declares your freedom from the tyranny of things and responsibilities.

A NEW VIEW OF SEXUALITY

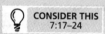 **CONSIDER THIS**
7:3–6

In an era when Greek women were often deprived both emotionally and sexually, Paul insisted that the Christian husband should recognize and fulfill the needs of his wife (vv. 3–6). He declared that marriage partners have authority over each other. That means that both husband and wife were forbidden from using sex as a means of control, but were to enjoy mutuality in that aspect of their marriage.

The gospel required a different understanding of sex and marriage than the surrounding culture's. Two thousand years later, it still does.

husband who does not believe, if he is willing to live with her, let her not divorce him. ¹⁴For the unbelieving husband is sanctified by the wife, and the unbelieving wife is sanctified by the husband; otherwise your children would be unclean, but now they are holy. ¹⁵But if the unbeliever departs, let him depart; a brother or a sister is not under bondage in such *cases.* But God has called us to peace. ¹⁶For how do you know, O wife, whether you will save *your* husband? Or how do you know, O husband, whether you will save *your* wife?

Calling and Vocation

7:17 ¹⁷But as God has distributed to each one, as the Lord has called each one, so let him walk. And so I ordain in all the churches. ¹⁸Was anyone called while circumcised? Let him not become uncircumcised. Was anyone called while uncircumcised? Let him not be circumcised. ¹⁹Circumcision is nothing and uncircumcision is nothing, but keeping the commandments of God *is what matters.* ²⁰Let each one remain in the same calling in which he was called. ²¹Were you called *while* a slave? Do not be concerned about it; but if you can be made free, rather use *it.* ²²For he who is called in the Lord *while* a slave is the Lord's freedman. Likewise he who is called *while* free is Christ's slave. ²³You were bought at a price; do not be-

CONSIDER THIS
7:17–24

CAREER CHANGES

Modern workers place a high value on mobility and freedom of choice. So how should Christians in our culture deal with Paul's admonition to remain in the situation where God has called us (vv. 17–24)? That sounds terribly antiquated in a society where the average person changes careers at least four times in life. In the ancient world, people normally worked for a lifetime at the same job.

Paul wrote that becoming a believer doesn't necessarily mean a career change. Wherever God has assigned us, that is our calling and we should pursue it to God's glory. On the other hand, there is nothing in the faith that locks a person into a work situation, any more than an unmarried woman must remain single all her life (7:8–9).

Paul's teaching about vocation parallels what he wrote about pre-conversion marriage (7:10–16). A believer is not compelled to leave his or her unbelieving spouse. On the other hand, the marriage may be dissolved if necessary to maintain peace. In the same way, believers should not use conversion as an excuse to leave their jobs.

7:17–24   come slaves of men. [24]Brethren, let each one remain with God in that *state* in which he was called.

Instructions Regarding Virgins

[25]Now concerning virgins: I have no commandment from the Lord; yet I give judgment as one whom the Lord in His mercy *has made* trustworthy. [26]I suppose therefore that this is good because of the present distress—that *it is* good for a man to remain as he is: [27]Are you bound to a wife? Do not seek to be loosed. Are you loosed from a wife? Do not seek a wife. [28]But even if you do marry, you have not sinned; and if a virgin marries, she has not sinned. Nevertheless such will have trouble in the flesh, but I would spare you.

[29]But this I say, brethren, the time *is* short, so that from now on even those who have wives should be as though they had none, [30]those who weep as though they did not weep, those who rejoice as though they did not rejoice, those who buy as though they did not possess, [31]and those who use this world as not misusing *it.* For the form of this world is passing away.

7:32–35
see pg. 592   [32]But I want you to be without care. He who is unmarried cares for the things of the Lord—how he may please the Lord. [33]But he who is married cares about the things of the world—how he may

* * *

This is an important point because Christianity introduces new values into our lives that may make us anxious to escape our work environment. The atmosphere of language and jokes, competition and politics, quotas and numbers may begin to feel uncomfortable. Wouldn't it be easier to quit one's job and go to work for a Christian employer—or better yet, pursue a career in a church or ministry? But Paul didn't encourage that choice as the normal path. A job change may be a possibility, as Jesus' disciples found out. But it is not necessarily virtuous to leave our "nets," especially if our only reason is to escape the realities of the work world. ◆

It's actually an advantage for us to work alongside unbelievers so that we can communicate the message of Christ by how we do our jobs. See "Your Workstyle," Titus 2:9–10.

QUOTE UNQUOTE

CONSIDER THIS
7:17   *Many believers today, like believers in Paul's day, struggle with how to bring their faith into their work. Should they quit their jobs and become vocational Christian workers? Paul did not encourage people to do that (v. 17). Here's a similar perspective from a twentieth-century believer:*

Look: the question is not whether we should bring God into our work or not. We certainly should and must: as Mac-Donald says, "All that is not God is death." The question is whether we should simply (a) bring Him in in the dedication of our work to Him, in the integrity, diligence, and humility with which we do it, or also (b) make His professed and explicit service our job. The A vocation rests on all men whether they know it or not; the B vocation only on those who are specially called to it. Each vocation has its peculiar dangers and peculiar rewards.

C.S. Lewis, Letter to Sheldon Vanauken, Jan. 8, 1951

GRAY AREAS

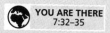

CONSIDER THIS
8:1–13

In first-century Corinth, meat sacrificed to idols (v. 1) proved to be an issue on which believers vehemently disagreed. It was a "gray" area of life, a matter for which there seemed to be no clear-cut instruction. How should Christians settle such disputes? Through a predetermined set of dos and don'ts? No, Paul offered a different perspective, one that appeals to conscience.

Paul argued that food and drink

(continued on next page)

please *his* wife. ³⁴There is*ᵃ* a difference between a wife and a virgin. The unmarried woman cares about the things of the Lord, that she may be holy both in body and in spirit. But she who is married cares about the things of the world—how she may please *her* husband. ³⁵And this I say for your own profit, not that I may put a leash on you, but for what is proper, and that you may serve the Lord without distraction.

³⁶But if any man thinks he is behaving improperly toward his virgin, if she is past the flower of youth, and thus it must be, let him do what he wishes. He does not sin; let them marry. ³⁷Nevertheless he who stands steadfast in his heart, having no necessity, but has power over his own will, and has so determined in his heart that he will keep his virgin,*ᵃ* does well. ³⁸So then he who gives *her*ᵃ in marriage does well, but he who does not give *her* in marriage does better.

7:34 ᵃM-Text adds *also.*   7:37 ᵃOr *virgin daughter*   7:38 ᵃNU-Text reads *his own virgin.*

YOU ARE THERE
7:32–35

WOMEN AND WORK IN THE ANCIENT WORLD

Paul's observation that a married woman must care about "the things of the world" (v. 34) hints at the busy lives that first century women lived, especially in the large cities of the Roman Empire.

The New Testament shows that women carried out a wide range of tasks: for example, drawing water, grinding grain, manufacturing tents, hosting guests, governing and influencing civic affairs, making clothes, teaching, prophesying and filling other spiritual functions, burying the dead, and doing the work of slaves, to name but a few. Additional evidence from the period reveals that women also served as wool workers, midwives, hairdressers, nurses, vendors, entertainers, political leaders, and even construction workers, among many other occupations.

If a woman was among the upper classes, she enjoyed relative economic security and social privileges. According to the Roman ideal, her role in society was to marry a citizen, produce legitimate heirs for him, and manage the household according to his orders. However, by the first century few families attained that ideal.

Wealthy women used slaves to perform such household tasks as cooking, making clothes, washing laundry, and caring for children (see "Children and Childcare," Matt. 19:14). Slaves also functioned as nurses, midwives, hairdressers, stenographers, and secretaries, and it was common for a high-ranking slave to be designated the household manager.

Instructions Regarding Remarriage

³⁹A wife is bound by law as long as her husband lives; but if her husband dies, she is at liberty to be married to whom she wishes, only in the Lord. ⁴⁰But she is happier if she remains as she is, according to my judgment—and I think I also have the Spirit of God.

CHAPTER 8

The Controversy of Meat Offered to Idols

8:1–13 ¹Now concerning things offered to idols: We know that we all have knowledge. Knowledge puffs up, but love edifies. ²And if anyone thinks that he knows anything, he knows nothing yet as he ought to know. ³But if anyone loves God, this one is known by Him.

⁴Therefore concerning the eating of things offered to

* * * * * * * * * * * * * * * *

Female slaves were not only considered to be household property, but sexual property as well. The master of the house could legally force a slave to have sex with him, or with anyone he chose. Any children that she bore became his property. In this way a citizen could increase his number of slaves.

Women who were former slaves, or freeborn, lacked the economic security of either the citizen or the slave. Nevertheless, many women sought to buy their way out of slavery. Some of these working-class women earned their living as vendors, selling fish, grain, vegetables, clothing, or perfume. Others became wet nurses, and some chose to become entertainers or prostitutes, occupations that were considered beneath the dignity of respectable women. ◆

In Jewish homes, women were responsible not only for carrying out household tasks, but also for preparing the home for the Sabbath. See "Jewish Homemaking," Mark 1:29–31.

Not all first-century women centered their lives around domestic responsibilities totally. Lydia was a successful businesswoman in the purple trade (see profile at Acts 16:14) and Priscilla manufactured tents with her husband (see profile at Rom. 16:3–5).

(continued from previous page)

do not determine our relationship to God (v. 8). Meat offered to idols is inconsequential because, ultimately, there is no such thing as an idol (vv. 4–6). An idol is not God, so the mere fact that a priest blesses meat and offers it to an idol means nothing. From that point of view, Christians should be able to enjoy whatever food they want.

However, questionable practices may affect one's relationships with fellow believers or unbelievers (v. 9). As members of Christ's family we are obligated not to be a "stumbling block," but a loving neighbor. Our faith is not merely private, but has a corporate ethic and public responsibility as well.

So we live in a tension: God's grace frees us to choose as we please, but God's love requires us to ask questions of conscience about our choices. From what we eat, to whom we live and work with, to where we live, to what we do with our money and time—almost everything we do affects our neighbors (vv. 10–13). So we need to ask, are we treating them with love?

We need not allow others to manipulate us through legalistic criticism. But we do need discretion as to how our choices affect those around us. It's not enough to follow Christ just in our hearts; we also need to follow Him in our consciences.

Several other principles that apply to these issues can be found in "Matters of Conscience," Rom. 14:1–23.

idols, we know that an idol is nothing in the world, and that *there is* no other God but one. ⁵For even if there are so-called gods, whether in heaven or on earth (as there are many gods and many lords), ⁶yet for us *there is* one God, the Father, of whom *are* all things, and we for Him; and one Lord Jesus Christ, through whom *are* all things, and through whom we *live*.

⁷However, *there is* not in everyone that knowledge; for some, with consciousness of the idol, until now eat *it* as a thing offered to an idol; and their conscience, being weak, is defiled. ⁸But food does not commend us to God; for neither if we eat are we the better, nor if we do not eat are we the worse.

⁹But beware lest somehow this liberty of yours become a stumbling block to those who are weak. ¹⁰For if anyone sees you who have knowledge eating in an idol's temple, will not the conscience of him who is weak be emboldened to eat those things offered to idols? ¹¹And because of your knowledge shall the weak brother perish, for whom Christ

---

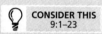

CONSIDER THIS
9:1–23

PAYING VOCATIONAL CHRISTIAN WORKERS

How much should pastors, missionaries, and others who work in churches and ministries be paid? Or should they be paid at all? Paul's example with the Corinthians offers some insight.

In Paul's day, philosophers traveled from city to city, teaching publicly for a fee. The more prestigious the teacher, the larger the fee. However, Paul charged the Corinthians nothing when he came and delivered the gospel message. As a result, some were criticizing him, asserting that he must not be an authentic leader of the church if he was rendering his services for free.

In reply, Paul explained himself (chapter 9). First, he insisted that those who labor spiritually should be supported materially by those with whom they work. He pointed to five familiar examples to support his position:

(1) Roman soldiers drew pay for their service (v. 7).
(2) Vintners enjoyed the fruits of their vineyards (v. 7).
(3) Shepherds received food from their flocks (v. 7).
(4) The Old Testament Law affirmed the right of laborers to receive fair compensation (vv. 8–10).
(5) The Law also allowed temple priests and attendants to live off of the sacrifices that the people brought (v. 13).

Paul also explained that the Lord Himself allowed those who preach the gospel to make their living from

died? 12But when you thus sin against the brethren, and wound their weak conscience, you sin against Christ. 13Therefore, if food makes my brother stumble, I will never again eat meat, lest I make my brother stumble.

CHAPTER 9

Paul's Own Example of Christian Liberty

9:1–23 1Am I not an apostle? Am I not free? Have I not seen Jesus Christ our Lord? Are you not my work in the Lord? 2If I am not an apostle to others, yet doubtless I am to you. For you are the seal of my apostleship in the Lord.

3My defense to those who examine me is this: 4Do we have no right to eat and drink? 5Do we have no right to take along a believing wife, as *do* also the other apostles, the brothers of the Lord, and Cephas? 9:6 6Or is it only Barnabas and I *who* have no right to refrain from working? 7Who ever goes to war at his own

♦ ♦ ♦ ♦ ♦ ♦ ♦ ♦ ♦ ♦ ♦ ♦ ♦ ♦ ♦ ♦ ♦

QUOTE UNQUOTE

CONSIDER THIS 9:6 *Paul had a right to be paid for preaching the gospel (v. 6), but he did not use that right (vv. 12, 15–17). Instead, he made his living as a tentmaker. Perhaps his training as a Pharisee encouraged him in that direction:*

Excellent is Torah study together with worldly business, for all Torah without work must ultimately fail and lead to sin.

Pirke Aboth ii:2

that occupation (v. 14). Elsewhere the apostle wrote that church elders who rule well are worthy of "double honor" (1 Tim. 5:17–18). The context shows that Paul had payment in mind. In short, effective vocational Christian workers should be paid fairly for their labor.

Yet Paul refused payment in Corinth. Why? Because He felt that he owed it to God to communicate the gospel for free. When he considered his past and how God had saved him, the "chief of sinners" (1 Tim. 1:15), it was payment enough to be able to tell people about Jesus (1 Cor. 9:18).

Should workers in churches and ministries be paid? This passage insists that they have a right to a fair wage, and Christians today do well to pay attention to Paul's words here in light of the many workers who are leaving the ministry because of inadequate support. On the other hand, Paul's example opens the door to an alternative—the idea of carrying out ministry for free while supporting oneself through other means. That is also a model worth considering in a day when, for a variety of reasons, an increasing number of churches and ministries are strapped for funds. ◆

RACERS' STARTING BLOCKS

THE GAMES

YOU ARE THERE 9:24–27 Paul's use of running, boxing, and other athletic feats (vv. 24–27) as metaphors for spiritual discipline was suited perfectly to the Corinthian culture. Corinth hosted numerous athletic events, including the prestigious Isthmian Games, one of four major athletic festivals of the Greeks.

The Isthmian Games were held every other year and attracted athletes from all over Greece. The competitions were between individuals, not teams, who vied more for glory than for tangible prizes. At the Corinthian games, victors were crowned with pine needle garlands, the "perishable crown" to which Paul referred (v. 25).

However, when the heroes returned home, their cities might erect statues in their honor, have a parade, and write poems celebrating their feats. Sometimes a champion was even exempted from paying taxes, given free meals, and placed in the seat of honor at public events.

(continued on next page)

expense? Who plants a vineyard and does not eat of its fruit? Or who tends a flock and does not drink of the milk of the flock?

⁸Do I say these things as a *mere* man? Or does not the law say the same also? ⁹For it is written in the law of Moses, "You shall not muzzle an ox while it treads out the grain."ᵃ Is it oxen God is concerned about? ¹⁰Or does He say *it* altogether for our sakes? For our sakes, no doubt, *this* is written, that he who plows should plow in hope, and he who threshes in hope should be partaker of his hope. ¹¹If we have sown spiritual things for you, *is it* a great thing if we reap your material things? ¹²If others are partakers of *this* right over you, *are* we not even more?

A Servant to All

Nevertheless we have not used this right, but endure all things lest we hinder the gospel of Christ. ¹³Do you not know that those who minister the holy things eat *of the things* of the temple, and those who serve at the altar partake of *the offerings of* the altar? ¹⁴Even so the Lord has commanded that those who preach the gospel should live from the gospel.

¹⁵But I have used none of these things, nor have I written these things that it should be done so to me; for it *would be* better for me to die than that anyone should make my boasting void. ¹⁶For if I preach the gospel, I have nothing to boast of, for necessity is laid upon me; yes, woe is me if I do not preach the gospel! ¹⁷For if I do this willingly, I have a reward; but if against my will, I have been entrusted with a stewardship. ¹⁸What is my reward then? That when I preach the gospel, I may present the gospel of Christᵃ without charge, that I may not abuse my authority in the gospel.

¹⁹For though I am free from all *men,* I have made myself a servant to all, that I might win the more; ²⁰and to the Jews I became as a Jew, that I might win Jews; to those *who are* under the law, as under the law,ᵃ that I might win those *who are* under the law; ²¹to those *who are* without law, as without law (not being without law toward God,ᵃ but under law toward Christᵇ), that I might win those *who are* without law; ²²to the weak I became asᵃ weak, that I might win the weak. I have become all things to all *men,* that I might by all means save some. ²³Now this I do for the gospel's sake, that I may be partaker of it with *you.*

9:24–27 ²⁴Do you not know that those who run in a race all run, but one receives the

9:9 ᵃDeuteronomy 25:4 9:18 ᵃNU-Text omits of Christ. 9:20 ᵃNU-Text adds though not being myself under the law. 9:21 ᵃNU-Text reads God's law. ᵇNU-Text reads Christ's law. 9:22 ᵃNU-Text omits as.

prize? Run in such a way that you may obtain *it*. ²⁵And everyone who competes *for the prize* is temperate in all things. Now they *do it* to obtain a perishable crown, but we *for* an imperishable *crown*. ²⁶Therefore I run thus: not with uncertainty. Thus I fight: not as *one who* beats the air. ²⁷But I discipline my body and bring *it* into subjection, lest, when I have preached to others, I myself should become disqualified.

CHAPTER 10

The Example of Israel

¹Moreover, brethren, I do not want you to be unaware that all our fathers were under the cloud, all passed through the sea, ²all were baptized into Moses in the cloud and in the sea, ³all ate the same spiritual food, ⁴and all drank the same spiritual drink. For they drank of that spiritual Rock that followed them, and that Rock was Christ. ⁵But with most of them God was not well pleased, for *their bodies* were scattered in the wilderness.

⁶Now these things became our examples, to the intent that we should not lust after evil things as they also lusted. ⁷And do not become idolaters as *were* some of them. As it is written, "The people sat down to eat and drink, and rose up to play."^a ⁸Nor let us commit sexual immorality, as some of them did, and in one day twenty-three thousand fell; ⁹nor let us tempt Christ, as some of them also tempted, and were destroyed by serpents; ¹⁰nor complain, as some of them also complained, and were destroyed by the destroyer. ¹¹Now all^a these things happened to them as examples, and they were written for our admonition, upon whom the ends of the ages have come.

10:12–13 see pg. 598 ¹²Therefore let him who thinks he stands take heed lest he fall. ¹³No temptation has overtaken you except such as is common to man; but God *is* faithful, who will not allow you to be tempted beyond what you are able, but with the temptation will also make the way of escape, that you may be able to bear *it*.

Flee from Idolatry

¹⁴Therefore, my beloved, flee from idolatry. ¹⁵I speak as to wise men; judge for yourselves what I say. ¹⁶The cup of blessing which we bless, is it not the communion of the blood of Christ? The bread which we break, is it not the communion of the body of Christ? ¹⁷For we, *though* many, are one bread *and* one body; for we all partake of that one bread.

(Bible text continued on page 599)

10:7 ^aExodus 32:6   10:11 ^aNU-Text omits *all*.

(continued from previous page)

One of the important institutions associated with these athletic contests was the *gymnasium*, where young men were educated by the philosophers and trained in various physical routines. The name derived from the fact that the athletes trained and performed naked (*gumnos*, "naked"). That and the fact that gymnastic activities were closely tied to Greek culture made the institution repulsive to most Jewish people. But Paul's Corinthian readers were no doubt well acquainted with this prominent part of Greek life.

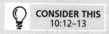
PAY ATTENTION TO TEMPTATION!

Paul's warning to "take heed lest [you] fall" (v. 12) is as necessary today as it has ever been. For we, like all who have gone before us, are fallen, temptable, and subject to thinking and doing what is wrong. Few teachings of Scripture have more practical implications for day-to-day living.

Opportunities for temptation are almost endless. And since human nature is not getting any better, nor is any of us immune to the corrupted appetites of the flesh, we need to take Paul's warning seriously and watch out for temptation, or we will surely fall. Yet Scripture offers several alternatives for dealing with temptation as we find it:

(1) We should *avoid* temptation whenever possible. Proverbs 4:14–15 urges us, "Do not enter the path of the wicked, and do not walk in the way of evil. Avoid it, do not travel on it." Often we know beforehand whether a certain set of circumstances is likely to lead to sin. Therefore, the obvious way to avoid sin is to avoid those circumstances. Paul described a "way of escape" from temptation (1 Cor. 10:13). Often the escape is to stay away from the place or the people where temptation lurks.

As believers, we can help others in this regard. We can avoid setting up situations that encourage people to do wrong. Teachers, for example, can help students avoid cheating by making assignments, giving tests, and communicating expectations in ways that reduce the need or incentive to cheat. Likewise, business owners and managers can devise procedures that don't needlessly place employees in a position where they might be tempted to steal cash, inventory, or equipment. It's not that a teacher or employer can't trust students or employees, but that no one can trust human nature to be immune from temptation.

(2) We should *flee* from powerful temptations. Earlier in this letter, Paul warned the Corinthians to flee sexual immorality (6:18). Here he warned them to flee idolatry (v. 14). Elsewhere he warned Timothy to flee the lust for material possessions and wealth (1 Tim. 6:9–11), as well as youthful lusts (2 Tim. 2:22). The message is clear: don't toy with temptation. Flee from it!

(3) Chronic temptation is something we need to *confess* and offer to Christ and ask for His cleansing work. Some temptations are powerful inner struggles, with thoughts and attitudes that graphically remind us of how fallen we really are. What should we do with that kind of temptation? Rather than deny it or try to repress it, we should bring it to Christ. He alone is capable of cleaning up the insides of our minds.

(4) Finally, we must *resist* temptation until it leaves us. When Christ was tempted by the devil, He resisted until the devil went away (Matt. 4:1–11). James encouraged us to do the same (James 4:7). Resistance begins by bathing our minds with the Word of God and standing our ground. We have the promise, after all, that the temptations we experience will never go beyond the common experiences of others, or beyond our ability to deal with them (1 Cor. 10:13). That is great news! ◆

¹⁸Observe Israel after the flesh: Are not those who eat of the sacrifices partakers of the altar? ¹⁹What am I saying then? That an idol is anything, or what is offered to idols is anything? ²⁰Rather, that the things which the Gentiles sacrifice they sacrifice to demons and not to God, and I do not want you to have fellowship with demons. ²¹You cannot drink the cup of the Lord and the cup of demons; you cannot partake of the Lord's table and of the table of demons. ²²Or do we provoke the Lord to jealousy? Are we stronger than He?

Do All to the Glory of God

²³All things are lawful for me,ᵃ but not all things are helpful; all things are lawful for me,ᵇ but not all things edify. ²⁴Let no one seek his own, but each one the other's *well-being.*

10:25–26 *see pg. 600* ²⁵Eat whatever is sold in the meat market, asking no questions for conscience' sake; ²⁶for "the earth *is* the LORD's, and all its fullness."ᵃ

²⁷If any of those who do not believe invites you *to dinner,* and you desire to go, eat whatever is set before you, asking no question for conscience' sake. ²⁸But if anyone says to you, "This was offered to idols," do not eat it for the sake of the one who told you, and for conscience' sake;ᵃ for "the earth *is* the LORD's, and all its fullness."ᵇ ²⁹"Conscience," I say, not your own, but that of the other. For why is my liberty judged by another *man's* conscience? ³⁰But if I partake with thanks, why am I evil spoken of for *the food* over which I give thanks?

³¹Therefore, whether you eat or drink, or whatever you do, do all to the glory of God. ³²Give no offense, either to the Jews or to the Greeks or to the church of God, ³³just as I also please all *men* in all *things,* not seeking my own profit, but the *profit* of many, that they may be saved.

CHAPTER 11

¹Imitate me, just as I also *imitate* Christ.

Head Coverings for Women

11:2–16

11:3 *see pg. 601* ²Now I praise you, brethren, that you remember me in all things and keep the traditions just as I delivered *them* to you. ³But I want you to know that the head of every man is Christ, the head of woman *is* man, and the head of Christ *is* God. ⁴Every man praying or prophesying, having *his* head covered, dishonors his head. ⁵But every

10:23 ᵃNU-Text omits *for me.*   ᵇNU-Text omits *for me.*   10:26 ᵃPsalm 24:1
10:28 ᵃNU-Text omits the rest of this verse.   ᵇPsalm 24:1

HEAD COVERINGS

CONSIDER THIS
11:2–16
Head coverings (vv. 4–6) were an important part of first-century wardrobes. Outdoors they provided both men and women protection from the intense sun and heat, as well as rain. In addition, a woman's head covering was a sign of modesty and commitment to her husband. Jewish and other women of the Near East wore veils in public, but Roman women never wore veils, and among the Greeks, some did and some did not. In some cultures, a woman without a veil was assumed to have loose morals.

These cultural issues came to bear on the women believers at Corinth. Controversy arose over whether they were required to keep their heads covered during worship or not. Paul wrote that the churches had no universal policy on the matter (v. 16), indicating that the women had some freedom to choose how they would handle the issue.

Observing the custom to wear a

(continued on next page)

(continued from previous page)

covering may have been especially important in Corinth, where a favorite slogan was, "Everything is permissible" (compare 1 Cor. 6:12; 10:23). Paul was eager for Christians to maintain a good reputation and give no cause for offense so that people hearing the gospel would have no barriers to becoming followers of Christ.

woman who prays or prophesies with *her* head uncovered dishonors her head, for that is one and the same as if her head were shaved. ⁶For if a woman is not covered, let her also be shorn. But if it is shameful for a woman to be shorn or shaved, let her be covered. ⁷For a man indeed ought not to cover *his* head, since he is the image and glory of God; but woman is the glory of man. ⁸For man is not from woman, but woman from man. ⁹Nor was man created for the woman, but woman for the man. ¹⁰For this reason the woman ought to have *a symbol of* authority on *her* head, because of the angels. ¹¹Nevertheless, neither *is* man independent of woman, nor woman independent of man, in the Lord. ¹²For as woman *came* from man, even so man also *comes* through woman; but all things are from God.

¹³Judge among yourselves. Is it proper for a woman to

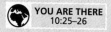

**YOU ARE THERE
10:25–26**

FOOD IN THE NEW TESTAMENT WORLD

Meat sold in the Corinthian meat market *(v. 25)* was meat that had been offered to the Greek gods. Thus Paul had to address the moral question of whether a believer in Christ should buy and eat such food. His conclusion: don't worry about it; the earth and all its products belong to God *(vv. 25–26)*.

Actually, **beef** was something of luxury in ancient Greece and seldom eaten on a regular basis. A far more common source of meat was **fish**. Other items in a typical meal might be **cheese, leeks, olives, wine, oil, and vinegar**. Greece raised some **wheat,** but most of its **bread** was made from imported grain from Egypt or Asia Minor.

In Palestine, the land of "milk and honey" (Ex. 13:5), Hebrew farmers raised a variety of cereal grains such as **wheat** and related products, **spelt, barley, and millet**. They also cultivated **cucumbers, squash, beans, lentils,**

pray to God with her head uncovered? ¹⁴Does not even nature itself teach you that if a man has long hair, it is a dishonor to him? ¹⁵But if a woman has long hair, it is a glory to her; for *her* hair is given to her*ᵃ* for a covering. ¹⁶But if anyone seems to be contentious, we have no such custom, nor *do* the churches of God.

Impropriety in Worship

¹⁷Now in giving these instructions I do not praise *you,* since you come together not for the better but for the worse. ¹⁸For first of all, when you come together as a church, I hear that there are divisions among you, and in

11:15 ᵃM-Text omits *to her.*

---

leeks, onions, and garlic. *Fruits and nuts included* **melons, grapes and raisins, figs, apricots, oranges, almonds, and pistachios**.

Honey *was gathered from bees or made from* **dates**. *Regional spices included* **mint, anise, dill, and cummin**. *As in the rest of the Mediterranean,* **olives** *were plentiful. They were eaten green or ripe, or they might be pressed into* **oil**, *which was used for cooking, seasoning, and as fuel for lamps.*

Beef and mutton *were a common part of the daily fare in Palestine, along with* **milk, butter, and cheese**. *A noon meal for a workman might consist of two small loaves of* **barley bread**—*one filled with cheese, the other with olives.*

Animals were divided into two classes by the Hebrews, clean and unclean (Lev. 11:1–47; Acts 10:9–15). Only **clean animals**—*those that chewed the cud and had divided hooves—could be used for food (Lev. 11:3), except the fat (Lev. 3:16–17). Pigs and camels were ceremonially unclean and therefore unfit for food.* **Camel's milk and cheese**, *however, were not forbidden.*

Many kinds of **fish** *could be eaten (Lev. 11:9–12), but not oysters or shrimp. Some twenty different species of* **birds** *were rejected (11:13–19). Insects that had legs and leaped, such as the* **grasshopper**, *were fit for consumption.*

The major preservative for these foods was **salt**. *An abundant supply was available from the Sea of Salt, or Dead Sea, in the south.* ◆

WHAT IS HEADSHIP?

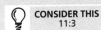 **CONSIDER THIS** 11:3 *What exactly did Paul mean when he used the word "head" (v. 3)? Some believe that the term by definition implies subordination of one person to another. Others disagree. For example, John Chrysostom, an early church leader, declared that only a heretic would understand "head" as chief or authority over. Rather, he understood the word as meaning absolute oneness, cause, or primal source.*

Either way, it's important to note that while "the head of Christ is God" (v. 3), Christ is elsewhere shown to be equal with God (for example, John 1:1–3; 10:30; Col. 1:15). So the term "head" need not exclude the idea of equality. At the same time, even though Christ is the equal of God, He became obedient to the point of death (Phil. 2:5–8), demonstrating that equality need not rule out submission.

part I believe it. ¹⁹For there must also be factions among you, that those who are approved may be recognized among you. ²⁰Therefore when you come together in one place, it is not to eat the Lord's Supper. ²¹For in eating, each one takes his own supper ahead of *others;* and one is hungry and another is drunk. ²²What! Do you not have houses to eat and drink in? Or do you despise the church of God and shame those who have nothing? What shall I say to you? Shall I praise you in this? I do not praise *you.*

The Proper Observance of the Lord's Supper

²³For I received from the Lord that which I also delivered to you: that the Lord Jesus on the *same* night in which He was betrayed took bread; ²⁴and when He had given thanks, He broke *it* and said, "Take, eat;ᵃ this is My body which is broken*ᵇ* for you; do this in remembrance of Me." ²⁵In the same manner *He* also

☑ **11:25**

11:24 ᵃNU-Text omits *Take, eat.*   ᵇNU-Text omits *broken.*

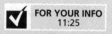

THE NEW COVENANT

Even a casual reader of the Bible soon discovers that it is divided into two major sections, the Old Testament and the New Testament. But how many readers realize that "testament" is just another word for "covenant"? Thus, the New Testament describes the new covenant (v. 25), or agreement, that God has made with humanity, based on the death and resurrection of Jesus Christ.

In the Bible, a covenant involves much more than a contract or simple agreement. A contract has an end date, but a covenant is a permanent arrangement. Furthermore, a contract generally involves only one aspect of a person, such as a skill, while a covenant covers a person's total being.

God entered into numerous covenants with people in the Old Testament. For example: with Adam and Eve (Gen. 3:15); with Noah (Gen. 8:21–22; 2 Pet. 3:7, 15); with Abraham (Gen. 12:1–3); with Israel (Deut. 29:1—30:20); and with David (2 Sam. 7:12–16; 22:51).

The agreement with Israel was especially significant, because it established a special relationship between God and the Hebrews. They were made His "chosen people" through whom He would bring blessing and hope to the rest of the world. However, because the recipients of God's Law could not keep it perfectly, further provision was necessary for them as well as for the rest of humanity.

That's why God promised a new covenant through the prophet Jeremiah (Jer. 31:31). Under the new covenant,

took the cup after supper, saying, "This cup is the new covenant in My blood. This do, as often as you drink *it*, in remembrance of Me."

26For as often as you eat this bread and drink this cup, you proclaim the Lord's death till He comes.

27Therefore whoever eats this bread or drinks *this* cup of the Lord in an unworthy manner will be guilty of the body and blood*a* of the Lord. 28But let a man examine himself, and so let him eat of the bread and drink of the cup. 29For he who eats and drinks in an unworthy manner*a* eats and drinks judgment to himself, not discerning the Lord's*b* body. 30For this reason many *are* weak and sick among you, and many sleep. 31For if we would judge ourselves, we would not be judged. 32But when we are judged, we are chastened by the Lord, that we may not be condemned with the world.

11:27 *a*NU-Text and M-Text read *the blood.* 11:29 *a*NU-Text omits *in an unworthy manner.* *b*NU-Text omits *Lord's.*

God would write His Law on human hearts. This suggested a new level of obedience and a new knowledge of the Lord.

The work of Jesus Christ brought the promised new covenant into being. When Jesus ate His final Passover meal with the Twelve, He spoke of the cup as "the new covenant in My blood" (Luke 22:20), the words that Paul quoted to the Corinthians to remind them of the need for purity and propriety in their worship (1 Cor. 11:25–34).

The new covenant in Jesus' blood rests directly on the sacrificial work of Christ on the cross (which was prefigured by Israel's system of sacrifices) and accomplishes the removal of sin and the cleansing of the conscience by faith in Him (Heb. 10:2, 22). So every time Christians celebrate the Lord's Supper, they remind themselves that God has fulfilled His promise: "I will be their God, and they shall be My people . . . I will be merciful to their unrighteousness, and their sins and their lawless deeds I will remember no more" (Heb. 8:10,12; compare Jer. 31:33–34). ◆

"**T**AKE, EAT; THIS IS MY BODY WHICH IS BROKEN FOR YOU."
—**1 Corinthians 11:24**

One of the striking features of God's covenant with Israel is that God is holy, all-knowing, and all-powerful, yet He consented to enter into a covenant with Abraham and his descendants—weak, sinful, and imperfect as they were. See "Israel," Rom. 10:1.

³³Therefore, my brethren, when you come together to eat, wait for one another. ³⁴But if anyone is hungry, let him eat at home, lest you come together for judgment. And the rest I will set in order when I come.

CHAPTER 12

The Spirit Gives Gifts to Each Believer

¹Now concerning spiritual *gifts*, brethren, I do not want you to be ignorant: ²You know thatᵃ you were Gentiles, carried away to these dumb idols, however you were led. ³Therefore I make known to you that no one speaking by the Spirit of God calls Jesus accursed, and no one can say that Jesus is Lord except by the Holy Spirit.

⁴There are diversities of gifts, but the same Spirit. ⁵There are differences of ministries, but the same Lord. ⁶And there are diversities of activities, but it is the same God who

12:2 ᵃNU-Text and M-Text add *when*.

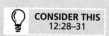

CONSIDER THIS
12:28–31

ARE SOME JOBS MORE IMPORTANT THAN OTHERS?

Does a hierarchy of gifts (vv. 28–31) mean God values some jobs more than others? Judging by popular opinion, one might conclude that He does. In fact, for centuries Christians have subscribed to a subtle yet powerful hierarchy of vocations.

In our culture, that hierarchy tends to position clergy (missionaries and evangelists, pastors and priests) at the top, members of the "helping professions" (doctors and nurses, teachers and educators, social workers) next, and "secular" workers (business executives, salespeople, factory laborers and farmers) at the bottom.

So what determines the spiritual value of a job? How does God assign significance? The hierarchy assumes sacred and secular distinctions, and assigns priority to the sacred. But does God view vocations that way?   No . . .

All legitimate work matters to God. *God Himself is a worker. In fact, human occupations find their origin in His work to create the world (Ps. 8:6–8). Work is a gift from Him to meet the needs of people and the creation.*

God creates people to carry out specific kinds of work. *God uniquely designs each of us, fitting us for certain kinds of tasks. He distributes skills, abilities, interests, and personalities among us so that we can carry out His work in the world. That work includes "spiritual" tasks, but also*

works all in all. [7]But the manifestation of the Spirit is given to each one for the profit *of all:* [8]for to one is given the word of wisdom through the Spirit, to another the word of knowledge through the same Spirit, [9]to another faith by the same Spirit, to another gifts of healings by the same[a] Spirit, [10]to another the working of miracles, to another prophecy, to another discerning of spirits, to another *different* kinds of tongues, to another the interpretation of tongues. [11]But one and the same Spirit works all these things, distributing to each one individually as He wills.

[12]For as the body is one and has many members, but all the members of that one body, being many, are one body, so also is Christ. [13]For by one Spirit we were all baptized into one body—whether Jews or Greeks, whether slaves or free—and have all been made to drink into[a] one Spirit. [14]For in fact the body is not one member but many.

12:9 [a]NU-Text reads *one.*   12:13 [a]NU-Text omits *into.*

extends to health, education, agriculture, business, law, communication, the arts, and so on.

God cares more about character and conduct than occupational status. *Paul's teaching in this passage is about gifts, not vocations. At the time Paul wrote it, there were few if any "professional" clergy in the church. Paul himself was a tentmaker by occupation, along with his friends, Aquila and Priscilla (1 Cor. 16:19; see Rom. 16:3–5). Other church leaders practiced a wide variety of professions and trades. God may assign rank among the spiritual gifts; but there's no indication that He looks at vocations that way.*

Furthermore, Scripture says there is something more important than gifts, "a more excellent way" (1 Cor. 12:31). Chapter 13 reveals it to be the way of Christlike love and character. Implication: If you want status in God's economy, excel at love, no matter what you do for work. Love has the greatest value to God (13:13; Matt. 22:35–40). ◆

Your work is like the work that God does, and it expresses something of who God is and what He wants done in the world. See "People at Work," Heb. 2:7.

Is it possible to hold a "secular" job and still seek the things of Christ? Or would it be better to quit and go into the ministry? See "The Spirituality of Everyday Work," Col. 3:1–2.

BY ONE
SPIRIT
WE WERE
ALL
BAPTIZED
INTO
ONE
BODY. . . .
—1 Corinthians 12:13

Every Member Is Necessary

15If the foot should say, "Because I am not a hand, I am not of the body," is it therefore not of the body? 16And if the ear should say, "Because I am not an eye, I am not of the body," is it therefore not of the body? 17If the whole body *were* an eye, where *would be* the hearing? If the whole *were* hearing, where *would be* the smelling? 18But now God has set the members, each one of them, in the body just as He pleased. 19And if they *were* all one member, where *would* the body *be?*

20But now indeed *there are* many members, yet one body. 21And the eye cannot say to the hand, "I have no need of you"; nor again the head to the feet, "I have no need of you." 22No, much rather, those members of the body which seem to be weaker are necessary. 23And those *members* of the body which we think to be less honorable, on these we bestow greater honor; and our unpresentable *parts* have greater modesty, 24but our presentable *parts* have no need. But God composed the body, having given greater honor to that *part* which lacks it, 25that there should be no schism in the body, but *that* the members should have the same care for one another. 26And if one member suffers, all the members suffer with *it;* or if one member is honored, all the members rejoice with *it.*

27Now you are the body of Christ, and members

12:28–31
see pg. 604

individually. 28And God has appointed these in the church: first

- -

A Lifestyle of Love

A CLOSER LOOK
13:1–13

In chapter 13, Paul described the lifestyle of love that Christ can produce in His followers. Elsewhere he painted a number of other pictures of what Christlikeness looks like. See "New Creatures with New Character," Gal. 5:22–23.

- -

Giving It All Away

A CLOSER LOOK
13:3

Just as the Love Chapter suggests (v. 3), Christ told one man to sell all of his possessions and give the proceeds to the poor (Mark 10:17–27). Apparently He felt that doing so would bring eternal profit to the man. But the fellow could not bear to part with his goods. At least he was honest enough to turn away, even if in sadness, rather than fake love and end up with nothing. See "The Man Who Had It All—Almost," Mark 10:17–27.

How should believers handle their money? See "Christians and Money," 1 Tim. 6:6–19.

apostles, second prophets, third teachers, after that miracles, then gifts of healings, helps, administrations, varieties of tongues. 29*Are* all apostles? *Are* all prophets? *Are* all teachers? *Are* all workers of miracles? 30Do all have gifts of healings? Do all speak with tongues? Do all interpret? 31But earnestly desire the best*a* gifts. And yet I show you a more excellent way.

CHAPTER 13

The Way of Love

13:1–13

1Though I speak with the tongues of men and of angels, but have not love, I have become sounding brass or a clanging cymbal. 2And though I have *the gift of* prophecy, and understand all mysteries and all knowledge, and though I have all faith, so that I could remove mountains, but have not love, I am

13:3

nothing. 3And though I bestow all my goods to feed *the poor,* and though I give my body to be burned,*a* but have not love, it profits me nothing.

4Love suffers long *and* is kind; love does not envy; love does not parade itself, is not puffed up; 5does not behave rudely, does not seek its own, is not provoked, thinks no evil; 6does not rejoice in iniquity, but rejoices in the truth; 7bears all things, believes all things, hopes all things, endures all things.

8Love never fails. But whether *there are* prophecies, they will fail; whether *there are* tongues, they will cease; whether *there is* knowledge, it will vanish away. 9For we know in part and we prophesy in part. 10But when that which is perfect has come, then that which is in part will be done away.

11When I was a child, I spoke as a child, I understood as a child, I thought as a child; but when I

13:12

became a man, I put away childish things. 12For now we see in a mirror, dimly, but then face to face. Now I know in part, but then I shall know just as I also am known.

13And now abide faith, hope, love, these three; but the greatest of these *is* love.

12:31 aNU-Text reads greater. 13:3 aNU-Text reads so I may boast.

CHAPTER 14

The Value of Prophecy

[1]Pursue love, and desire spiritual *gifts,* but especially that you may prophesy. [2]For he who speaks in a tongue does not speak to men but to God, for no one understands *him;* however, in the spirit he speaks mysteries. [3]But he who prophesies speaks edification and exhortation and comfort to men. [4]He who speaks in a tongue edifies himself, but he who prophesies edifies the church. [5]I wish you all spoke with tongues, but even more that you prophesied; for[a] he who prophesies *is* greater than he who speaks with tongues, unless indeed he interprets, that the church may receive edification.

[6]But now, brethren, if I come to you speaking with tongues, what shall I profit you unless I speak to you either by revelation, by knowledge, by prophesying, or by teaching? [7]Even things without life, whether flute or harp, when they make a sound, unless they make a distinction in the sounds, how will it be known what is piped or played? [8]For if the trumpet makes an uncertain sound, who will prepare for battle? [9]So likewise you, unless you utter by the tongue words easy to understand, how will it be known what is spoken? For you will be speaking into the air. [10]There are, it may be, so many kinds of languages in the world, and none of them *is* without significance. [11]Therefore, if I do not know the meaning of the language, I shall be a foreigner to him who speaks, and he who speaks *will be* a foreigner to me. [12]Even so you, since you are zealous for spiritual *gifts, let it be* for the edification of the church *that* you seek to excel.

The Reason for Tongues

[13]Therefore let him who speaks in a tongue pray that he may interpret. [14]For if I pray in a tongue, my spirit prays, but my understanding is unfruitful. [15]What is *the conclusion* then? I will pray with the spirit, and I will also pray with the understanding. I will sing with the spirit, and I will also sing with the understanding. [16]Otherwise, if you bless with the spirit, how will he who occupies the place of the uninformed say "Amen" at your giving of thanks, since he does not understand what you say? [17]For you indeed give thanks well, but the other is not edified.

[18]I thank my God I speak with tongues more than you all; [19]yet in the church I would rather speak five words with my understanding, that I may teach others also, than ten thousand words in a tongue.

[20]Brethren, do not be children in understanding; however, in malice be babes, but in understanding be mature.

14:5 [a]NU-Text reads *and.*

NOT PERMITTED TO SPEAK?

 CONSIDER THIS
14:34

When Paul writes that women should keep silent in the churches (v. 34), we are led to ask why in light of previous statements in the letter. He has already mentioned that women prayed and prophesied, presumably during worship services (11:5). Likewise, he has written that the Spirit gave gifts to everyone in the body (12:7, 11), and presumably some of the women received some of the speaking gifts. So why would he exhort the women to keep silent?

One explanation is that the women in the congregation at Corinth probably had few opportunities for formal education and little exposure to large gatherings—except for the wild rites of their former religion. So when they came into the church, they may have assumed a similar approach to Christian worship. That would have been inappropriate, so Paul exhorted them to pursue a quieter, more orderly form of worship now that they were following the Lord.

²¹In the law it is written:

"With *men of* other tongues and other lips
  I will speak to this people;
  And yet, for all that, they will not hear Me,"ᵃ

says the Lord.

²²Therefore tongues are for a sign, not to those who believe but to unbelievers; but prophesying is not for unbelievers but for those who believe. ²³Therefore if the whole church comes together in one place, and all speak with tongues, and there come in *those who are* uninformed or unbelievers, will they not say that you are out of your mind? ²⁴But if all prophesy, and an unbeliever or an uninformed person comes in, he is convinced by all, he is convicted by all. ²⁵And thusᵃ the secrets of his heart are revealed; and so, falling down on *his* face, he will worship God and report that God is truly among you.

Order in Worship

²⁶How is it then, brethren? Whenever you come together, each of you has a psalm, has a teaching, has a tongue, has a revelation, has an interpretation. Let all things be done for edification. ²⁷If anyone speaks in a tongue, *let there be* two or at the most three, *each* in turn, and let one interpret. ²⁸But if there is no interpreter, let him keep silent in church, and let him speak to himself and to God. ²⁹Let two or three prophets speak, and let the others judge. ³⁰But if *anything* is revealed to another who sits by, let the first keep silent. ³¹For you can all prophesy one by one, that all may learn and all may be encouraged. ³²And the spirits of the prophets are subject to the prophets. ³³For God is not *the author* of confusion but of peace, as in all the churches of the saints.

 14:34 ³⁴Let yourᵃ women keep silent in the churches, for they are not permitted to speak; but *they are* to be submissive, as the law also says. ³⁵And if they want to learn something, let them ask their own husbands at home; for it is shameful for women to speak in church.

³⁶Or did the word of God come *originally* from you? Or *was it* you only that it reached? ³⁷If anyone thinks himself to be a prophet or spiritual, let him acknowledge that the things which I write to you are the commandments of the Lord. ³⁸But if anyone is ignorant, let him be ignorant.ᵃ

³⁹Therefore, brethren, desire earnestly to prophesy, and do not forbid to speak with tongues. ⁴⁰Let all things be done decently and in order.

14:21 ᵃIsaiah 28:11, 12   14:25 ᵃNU-Text omits *And thus.*   14:34 ᵃNU-Text omits *your.*
14:38 ᵃNU-Text reads *if anyone does not recognize this, he is not recognized.*

CHAPTER 15

What the Gospel Is

¹Moreover, brethren, I declare to you the gospel which I preached to you, which also you received and in which you stand, ²by which also you are saved, if you hold fast that word which I preached to you—unless you believed in vain.

³For I delivered to you first of all that which I also received: that Christ died for our sins according to the Scriptures, ⁴and that He was buried, and that He rose again the third day according to the Scriptures, ⁵and that He was seen by Cephas, then by the twelve. ⁶After that He was seen by over five hundred brethren at once, of whom the greater part remain to the present, but some have fallen asleep. ⁷After that He was seen by James, then by all the apostles. ⁸Then last of all He was seen by me also, as by one born out of due time.

15:9–10
see pg. 610

⁹For I am the least of the apostles, who am not worthy to be called an apostle, because I persecuted the church of God. ¹⁰But by the grace of God I am what I am, and His grace toward me was not in vain; but I labored more abundantly than they all, yet not I, but the grace of God *which was* with me. ¹¹Therefore, whether *it was* I or they, so we preach and so you believed.

Who Says There Is No Resurrection?

¹²Now if Christ is preached that He has been raised from the dead, how do some among you say that there is no resurrection of the dead? ¹³But if there is no resurrection of the dead, then Christ is not risen. ¹⁴And if Christ is not risen, then our preaching *is* empty and your faith *is* also empty. ¹⁵Yes, and we are found false witnesses of God, because we have testified of God that He raised up Christ, whom He did not raise up—if in fact the dead do not rise. ¹⁶For if *the* dead do not rise, then Christ is not risen. ¹⁷And if Christ is not risen, your faith *is* futile; you are still in your sins! ¹⁸Then also those who have fallen asleep in Christ have perished. ¹⁹If in this life only we have hope in Christ, we are of all men the most pitiable.

²⁰But now Christ is risen from the dead, *and* has become the firstfruits of those who have fallen asleep. ²¹For since by man *came* death, by Man also *came* the resurrection of the dead. ²²For as in Adam all die, even so in Christ all shall be made alive. ²³But each one in his own order: Christ the firstfruits, afterward those *who are* Christ's at His coming.

15:24

²⁴Then *comes* the end, when He delivers the kingdom to God the Father, when He

(Bible text continued on page 611)

THE END OF AUTHORITY

CONSIDER THIS
15:24

Someday all authority, rule, and power will end—a sobering thought (v. 24). Peter mentioned a similar idea when he asked, in light of the end of the present time, what sort of people should we be (1 Pet. 3:10–13)? How should we live? No matter how hard we've worked to acquire and accrue power and position, it will eventually come to an end. That thought should challenge us to hold on lightly to the trappings of authority and use it wisely and responsibly for God's purposes.

MYTH: PEOPLE BECOME CHRISTIANS THROUGH SOCIAL CONDITIONING

Many people today accept a number of myths about Christianity, with the result that they never respond to Jesus as He really is. This is one of ten articles that speak to some of those misconceptions. For a list of all ten, see 1 Tim. 1:3–4.

Paul's statement that he persecuted the church prior to his conversion (vv. 9–10) is a strong piece of evidence against the commonly held notion that religious preference is mainly a result of upbringing.

Without question, cultural circumstances play a part in people's religious beliefs. A Hindu background would tend to predispose a person towards Hinduism, a Christian background toward Christianity, and so forth. But can social conditioning alone explain why people believe and behave as they do? After all, a Christian upbringing is no guarantee that a person won't someday abandon the faith. On the other hand, countless people who have had no exposure to Christianity in their youth nevertheless convert as adults.

The fact is, Christian conversion is much misunderstood. It is often regarded as sudden, irrational, selective, and even illusory. But what are its essential elements? Paul's experience is instructive. While certain aspects of his conversion were unique, four elements stand out that are present in every authentic conversion:

(1) *His conversion touched his conscience.* He recognized that he had been fighting God and that his vicious treatment of Christians was wrong (Acts 26:9–11; 1 Tim. 1:13).

(2) *His conversion touched his understanding.* He discovered that the Jesus he was persecuting was no less than the risen Messiah, the Son of God (Acts 9:22).

(3) *His conversion touched his will.* He gave in to Jesus and began following Him (Acts 26:19–20).

(4) *His conversion produced noticeable change in his life.* His ambitions, his character, his relationships, his outlook— everything changed as a result of his encounter with Christ (Phil. 3:7–11).

But suppose, as some have, that it all amounts to nothing but an illusion? Three tests can be applied to determine whether religious experience in general and Christianity in particular is illusory. First, there is the test of history. Christianity makes historical claims. Are those claims valid? Does history bear them out? Yes it does. There is nothing illusory about Jesus or His impact on the world. Nor are His claims illusory (see "Myth #1: Jesus Christ Was Only a Great Moral Teacher," Matt. 13:34–35). Likewise, His death and resurrection are well attested (see "Myth #2: There Is No Evidence That Jesus Rose From the Dead," Matt. 28:1–10). Nor is there any doubt about the reality of the church. In short, Christian faith is rooted in historical fact.

A second test is the test of character. When drunkards become sober and crooks become honest, when animists give up their mysticism and people enslaved by black magic are set free, when self-centered people become generous and unbelievers become giants of faith, it is very difficult to explain it away as illusion. Changed lives are not the only evidence of Christianity's authenticity, but they are certainly an impressive one.

(continued on next page)

puts an end to all rule and all authority and power. ²⁵For He must reign till He has put all enemies under His feet. ²⁶The last enemy *that* will be destroyed *is* death. ²⁷For "He has put all things under His feet."ᵃ But when He says "all things are put under *Him*," *it is* evident that He who put all things under Him is excepted. ²⁸Now when all things are made subject to Him, then the Son Himself will also be subject to Him who put all things under Him, that God may be all in all.

²⁹Otherwise, what will they do who are baptized for the dead, if the dead do not rise at all? Why then are they baptized for the dead? ³⁰And why do we stand in jeopardy every hour? ³¹I affirm, by the boasting in you which I have in Christ Jesus our Lord, I die daily. ³²If, in the manner of men, I have fought with beasts at Ephesus, what advantage *is it* to me? If *the* dead do not rise, "Let us eat and drink, for tomorrow we die!"ᵃ

³³Do not be deceived: "Evil company corrupts good habits." ³⁴Awake to righteousness, and do not sin; for some do not have the knowledge of God. I speak *this* to your shame.

A New Body

³⁵But someone will say, "How are the dead raised up? And with what body do they come?" ³⁶Foolish one, what you sow is not made alive unless it dies. ³⁷And what you sow, you do not sow that body that shall be, but mere grain—perhaps wheat or some other *grain*. ³⁸But God gives it a body as He pleases, and to each seed its own body.

³⁹All flesh *is* not the same flesh, but *there is* one *kind of* fleshᵃ of men, another flesh of animals, another of fish, *and* another of birds.

⁴⁰*There are* also celestial bodies and terrestrial bodies; but the glory of the celestial *is* one, and the *glory* of the terrestrial *is* another. ⁴¹*There is* one glory of the sun, another glory of the moon, and another glory of the stars; for *one* star differs from *another* star in glory.

15:42
see pg. 612
⁴²So also *is* the resurrection of the dead. *The body* is sown in corruption, it is raised in incorruption. ⁴³It is sown in dishonor, it is raised in glory. It is sown in weakness, it is raised in power. ⁴⁴It is sown a natural body, it is raised a spiritual body. There is a natural body, and there is a spiritual body. ⁴⁵And so it is written, "The first man Adam became a living being."ᵃ The last Adam *became* a life-giving spirit.

⁴⁶However, the spiritual is not first, but the natural, and afterward the spiritual. ⁴⁷The first man *was* of the earth,

(Bible text continued on page 613)

MYTH #6
10 MYTHS ABOUT CHRISTIANITY

(continued from previous page)

Finally there is the test of power. Delusions and neuroses tend to destroy people's character. They produce unbalanced behavior and keep people from achieving their goals. Christianity has precisely the opposite effect. It makes people whole. It even enables people to face death—a time when delusions are usually stripped away—with confidence and courage.

History, character, power: these cannot be attributed to social conditioning. Rather they strongly suggest that something far deeper lies behind Christianity, something good, powerful, and alive. ◆

BURIAL

Paul's doctrine of the resurrection (v. 42) flew in the face of prevailing ideas about the afterlife. To the Greek mind, death released a person's spirit from the prison of the body. The last thing a Greek would want was to be reunited with a corruptible body (v. 35).

Burial practices in Corinth and the other cities of the Roman Empire were largely a function of one's status in life. If the deceased was a member of the upper classes, the job of preparing the body was delegated to professional undertakers. They usually dressed the body in a toga adorned with badges and other tokens of the person's accomplishments and offices. Professional mourners and musicians then led a funeral procession to the burial site. Sometimes actors were recruited to follow the cortege, wearing masks that depicted the family's ancestors.

In Greek and Roman cultures, bodies were as likely to be cremated as buried. Either way, the rich tended to bury their dead in elaborate tombs. Some even

formed cooperatives in which hundreds of urns were placed.

The poor, by contrast, laid their dead to rest in common, often unmarked graves. Or, if they lived in or near Rome, they might use the catacombs, a maze of underground tunnels outside the city. In the later years of the first century, Christians were not permitted to use regular cemeteries, so they resorted to the catacombs for their funerals. As persecution increased, some eventually fled there for survival.

Among the Hebrews, bodies were laid either in a shallow grave covered with stones or in a cave or tomb hewn out of stone and secured by a circular stone rolled and sealed over the entrance. Graves were often

marked with a large, upright stone.

Due to the hot climate of Palestine, dead bodies decayed rapidly, so burial usually took place within a few hours after death. If someone died late in the day, burial took place the next day, but always within twenty-four hours after death.

The Hebrews did not follow the Greek custom of cremation, except in emergencies, nor did they generally use coffins. And even though they had historical ties to Egypt, they did not embalm their dead as the Egyptians did.

Mummification was invented by the Egyptians more than 3,000 years ago. They believed that the preservation of the body insured the continuation of the soul after death.

According to the Greek historian Herodotus, there were three different methods of embalming. The least expensive method involved emptying the intestines by flushing them with a cleaning

(continued on next page)

made of dust; the second Man *is* the Lord[a] from heaven. [48]As *was* the *man* of dust, so also *are* those *who are* made of dust; and as *is* the heavenly *Man,* so also *are* those *who are* heavenly. [49]And as we have borne the image of the *man* of dust, we shall also bear[a] the image of the heavenly *Man.*

[50]Now this I say, brethren, that flesh and blood cannot inherit the kingdom of God; nor does corruption inherit incorruption. [51]Behold, I tell you a mystery: We shall not all sleep, but we shall all be changed— [52]in a moment, in the twinkling of an eye, at the last trumpet. For the trumpet will sound, and the dead will be raised incorruptible, and we shall be changed. [53]For this corruptible must put on incorruption, and this mortal *must* put on immortality. [54]So when this corruptible has put on incorruption, and this mortal has put on immortality, then shall be brought to pass the saying that is written: "Death is swallowed up in victory."[a]

[55] "O Death, where *is* your sting?[a]
    O Hades, where *is* your victory?"[b]

[56]The sting of death *is* sin, and the strength of sin *is* the law. [57]But thanks *be* to God, who gives us the victory through our Lord Jesus Christ.

[58]Therefore, my beloved brethren, be steadfast, immovable, always abounding in the work of the Lord, knowing that your labor is not in vain in the Lord.

CHAPTER 16

A Collection for Believers at Jerusalem

16:1–4
see pg. 615
[1]Now concerning the collection for the saints, as I have given orders to the churches of Galatia, so you must do also: [2]On the first *day* of the week let each one of you lay something aside, storing up as he may prosper, that there be no collections when I come. [3]And when I come, whomever you approve by *your* letters I will send to bear your gift to Jerusalem. [4]But if it is fitting that I go also, they will go with me.

[5]Now I will come to you when I pass through Macedonia (for I am passing through Macedonia). [6]And it may be that I will remain, or even spend the winter with you, that you may send me on my journey, wherever I go. [7]For I do not wish to see you now on the way; but I hope to stay a while with you, if the Lord permits.

16:9–20
see pg. 614
[8]But I will tarry in Ephesus until Pentecost. [9]For a great and effective door has opened to me, and *there are* many adversaries.

15:47 [a]NU-Text omits *the Lord.*   15:49 [a]M-Text reads *let us also bear.*   15:54 [a]Isaiah 25:8
15:55 [a]Hosea 13:14   [b]NU-Text reads *O Death, where is your victory? O Death, where is your sting?*

(continued from previous page)

liquid, after which the body was soaked in natron. A second method called for placing the body in natron after the stomach and intestines had been dissolved by an injection of cedar oil.

The most elaborate method of embalming required the removal of the brain and all internal organs except the heart. The inner cavity of the body was then washed and filled with spices. The corpse was soaked in natron, then washed and wrapped in bandages of linen soaked with gum. Finally, the embalmed body was placed in a wooden coffin. These processes proved remarkably effective in preserving bodies from decay. ◆

Among Jews at the time of Christ, it was chiefly the women's task to prepare bodies for interment. See the article, "Funeral Preparations," John 12:1–8.

Greetings and Conclusion

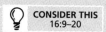

16:10

¹⁰And if Timothy comes, see that he may be with you without fear; for he does the work of the Lord, as I also *do*. ¹¹Therefore let no one despise him. But send him on his journey in peace, that he may come to me; for I am waiting for him with the brethren.

¹²Now concerning *our* brother Apollos, I strongly urged him to come to you with the brethren, but he was quite unwilling to come at this time; however, he will come when he has a convenient time.

¹³Watch, stand fast in the faith, be brave, be strong. ¹⁴Let all *that* you *do* be done with love.

¹⁵I urge you, brethren—you know the household of Stephanas, that it is the firstfruits of Achaia, and *that* they have devoted themselves to the ministry of the saints—

Timothy

A CLOSER LOOK
16:10

Timothy (v. 10) was one of Paul's most trusted and valued companions. To find out more about this promising young man, see his profile at the Introduction to 1 and 2 Timothy.

CONSIDER THIS
16:9–20

ENEMIES BECOME FAMILY AND FRIENDS

Paul had once been a dangerous enemy to the followers of Christ. But his dramatic encounter with the Savior and subsequent change of heart brought him into the family of God (Acts 9:1–30). Courageous Christians such as Ananias (see 9:10) and Barnabas (see 4:36–37) began to nurture and aid the new believer. He had become a brother.

In the same way, Christ makes believers today into a new family. Having experienced the same gift from God—forgiveness and hope—we are now brothers and sisters in Christ.

Paul acknowledged several of his family of faith as he closed 1 Corinthians:

- *Young* Timothy (1 Cor. 16:10–11), who needed acceptance and affirmation (see Timothy's profile at the Introduction to 1 and 2 Timothy).
- *Gifted* Apollos (v. 12), one of the Corinthians' former leaders (1:12) who was unable to go to them at that time (see "Apollos," Acts 18:24–28).
- *Stephanas* (vv. 15–16), baptized by Paul in the early days of the Corinthian church; the Corinthians needed to respect him.

16that you also submit to such, and to everyone who works and labors with us.

17I am glad about the coming of Stephanas, Fortunatus, and Achaicus, for what was lacking on your part they supplied. 18For they refreshed my spirit and yours. Therefore acknowledge such men.

16:19 19The churches of Asia greet you. Aquila and Priscilla greet you heartily in the Lord, with the church that is in their house. 20All the brethren greet you.

Greet one another with a holy kiss.

21The salutation with my own hand—Paul's.

22If anyone does not love the Lord Jesus Christ, let him be accursed.a O Lord, come!b

23The grace of our Lord Jesus Christ be with you. 24My love be with you all in Christ Jesus. Amen.

16:22 aGreek anathema bAramaic Maranatha

Aquila and Priscilla

A CLOSER LOOK 16:19 *Aquila and Priscilla (v. 19) were old friends of the Corinthians. In fact, they had been instrumental in starting the church at Corinth (Acts 18:1–11). To find out more about these valuable coworkers, business partners, and friends of Paul, see their profile at Rom. 16:3–5.*

- *Fortunatus and Achaicus (vv. 17–18), encouragers of Paul who may have delivered to him the letter from the Corinthians that he was answering with 1 Corinthians; like Stephanas, they too needed recognition.*
- *Priscilla and Aquila (v. 19), co-founders of the Corinthian work and business partners with Paul (Acts 18:1–4); they now were leading a similar work at Ephesus and sent warm greetings to their brothers and sisters across the "wine dark" Aegean Sea (see "Priscilla and Aquila," Rom. 16:3–5).*

Once an enemy, Paul became a true friend, partner, and advocate of other believers. Just as others had once cared for him and his needs, he wrote to the Corinthians of the needs and concerns of his brothers and sisters in Christ.

Who are some of your friends in the faith? Who among them needs support or advocacy right now? To whom can you appeal on their behalf? ◆

MONEY: COMPASSION AND INTEGRITY

CONSIDER THIS 16:1–4 **Money is powerful. It can bring out the best or the worst in a person. In our drive to gain lots of it or use it for personal comfort and convenience, we can become very cold and manipulative (1 Tim. 6:10). But that ought not to be the way for God's followers.**

In 1 Corinthians 16, we see that Paul was coordinating a fund-raising drive to help some needy believers. He could have focused on the plight of the recipients. They were Christians in Jerusalem, perhaps suffering from persecution or famine. But instead he concentrated on how the Corinthians should initiate a regular pattern of giving to meet the need (1 Cor. 16:2). Their participation would be an act of loving worship as they met together on the first day of the week.

Paul also pointed out that the transfer of the funds would be carried out by responsible people chosen by the Corinthians themselves (v. 3). That guaranteed accountability and integrity. Apparently Paul was quite realistic about the human tendency toward manipulation and greed.

How are you using your money to alleviate suffering and meet the needs of others?

God is as interested in what Christians do with the money they keep as He is in the money they give away. See "Christians and Money," 1 Tim. 6:6–19.

2 Corinthians

CONTENTS

Integrity In the Face of Competition (10:1)

When you face a competitive situation, are you tempted to do *whatever* it takes to win? Or can you keep the big picture, avoiding short-term gains in order to live with long-term, Christlike values?

When I Am Weak, Then I Am Strong (12:7–10)

It's hard to believe and it flies in the face of our culture's way of thinking, but weakness can make a person strong.

Spiritual Authority (13:10)

Anyone who exercises leadership among other believers will want to carefully study Paul's use of authority.

CORINTH

- **A major city of Greece situated on the Isthmus of Corinth between the Ionian Sea and the Aegean Sea.**
- **In New Testament times, perhaps the most celebrated city of the Roman Empire, second only to Rome.**
- **Less than 100 years old at the time of Paul.**
- **A "planned" city rebuilt from ashes by the Roman emperors.**
- **A transportation hub for both land and sea travel. Though not a seaport, its location on an isthmus linked two seaports and two bays. To save time and avoid potential disasters of sailing around Greece, shippers transported passengers and their goods across the isthmus and reloaded them onto ships on the other side.**
- **Greece's leading commercial center for trade, agriculture, and industry.**
- **Host city to numerous athletic events, gladiatorial contests, theater productions, and the Isthmian Games, one of four major athletic festivals of the Greeks.**
- **A major center for pagan religions. More than twelve temples have been excavated at Corinth, including the magnificent temple of Apollo, with its 38 Doric columns 24 feet high. The temple of Aphrodite, goddess of love, employed at least 1,000 temple prostitutes. The city had a widespread reputation for gross immorality.**
- **A city of diverse peoples and cultures, including Greeks, Roman colonists (mostly retired army veterans and freedmen), and Jews, some of whom migrated there during persecution under the emperor Claudius (Acts 18:1).**

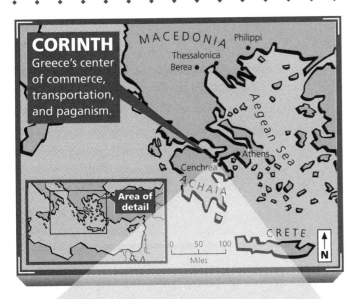

CORINTH Greece's center of commerce, transportation, and paganism.

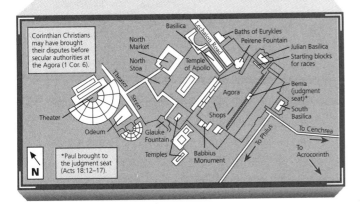

The Corinthians were first-century Christians but they struggled with a number of twenty-first-century problems. See the Introduction to 1 and 2 Corinthians.

CHAPTER 1

Comfort in the Midst of Trouble

¹Paul, an apostle of Jesus Christ by the will of God, and Timothy *our* brother,

To the church of God which is at Corinth, with all the saints who are in all Achaia:

²Grace to you and peace from God our Father and the Lord Jesus Christ.

³Blessed *be* the God and Father of our Lord Jesus Christ, the Father of mercies and God of all comfort, ⁴who comforts us in all our tribulation, that we may be able to comfort those who are in any trouble, with the comfort with which we ourselves are comforted by God. ⁵For as the sufferings of Christ abound in us, so our consolation also abounds through Christ. ⁶Now if we are afflicted, *it is* for your consolation and salvation, which is effective for enduring the same sufferings which we also suffer. Or if we are comforted, *it is* for your consolation and salvation. ⁷And our hope for you *is* steadfast, because we know that as you are partakers of the sufferings, so also *you will partake* of the consolation.

⁸For we do not want you to be ignorant, brethren, of our trouble which came to us in Asia: that we were burdened beyond measure, above strength, so that we despaired even of life. ⁹Yes, we had the sentence of death in ourselves, that we should not trust in ourselves but in God who raises the dead, ¹⁰who

YOU
OUGHT
RATHER
TO
FORGIVE
AND
COMFORT. . . .
—2 Corinthians 2:7

ASIA MINOR

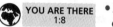

YOU ARE THERE 1:8 • A peninsula, also called Anatolia, situated in the extreme western part of the continent of Asia.
• Bounded on the north by the Black Sea, the Sea of Marmara, and the Dardanelles; the Aegean Sea on the west; and Syria and the Mediterranean Sea on the south.
• Roughly identical with the modern nation of Turkey.
• A high plateau crossed by mountains, especially the Taurus Mountains near the southern coast.
• In the New Testament, the term "Asia" is ambiguous, sometimes referring to the peninsula of Asia Minor as a whole (Acts 19:26–27), but more often referring to proconsular Asia, situated in the western part of the peninsula (Acts 2:9; 6:9).

The explosive impact of the gospel at Ephesus reverberated throughout Asia Minor, such that "all who dwelt in Asia heard the word of the Lord Jesus" (Acts 19:10). See "The Ephesus Approach," Acts 19:8–41.

DACIA

MOESIA

MACEDONIA

THRACE

Black Sea

COLCHIS

ARMENIA

BITHYNIA
PONTUS

MYSIA
PHRYGIA
GALATIA
CAPPADOCIA

ASIA
PISIDIA
LYCAONIA

Tigris River

ACHAIA

Aegean Sea

LYCIA
PAMPHYLIA
CILICIA

MESOPOTAMIA

Euphrates River

CRETE

RHODES

CYPRUS

SYRIA

Mediterranean Sea

ARABIA

0   100   200
Miles

N

delivered us from so great a death, and does[a] deliver us; in whom we trust that He will still deliver *us*, 11you also helping together in prayer for us, that thanks may be given by many persons on our[a] behalf for the gift *granted* to us through many.

Paul Defends His Integrity

12For our boasting is this: the testimony of our conscience that we conducted ourselves in the world in simplicity and godly sincerity, not with fleshly wisdom but by the grace of God, and more abundantly toward you. 13For we are not writing any other things to you than what you read or understand. Now I trust you will understand, even to the end 14(as also you have understood us in part), that we are your boast as you also *are* ours, in the day of the Lord Jesus.

Paul Explains His Plans

15And in this confidence I intended to come to you before, that you might have a second benefit— 16to pass by way of you to Macedonia, to come again from Macedonia to you, and be helped by you on my way to Judea. 17Therefore, when I was planning this, did I do it lightly? Or the things I plan, do I plan according to the flesh, that with me there should be Yes, Yes, and No, No? 18But *as* God is faithful, our word to you was not Yes and No.

1:19–20 19For the Son of God, Jesus Christ, who was preached among you by us—by me, Silvanus, and Timothy —was not Yes and No, but in Him was Yes. 20For all the promises of God in Him *are* Yes, and in Him Amen, to the glory of God through us. 21Now He who establishes us with you in Christ and has anointed us *is* God, 22who also has sealed us and given us the Spirit in our hearts as a guarantee.

23Moreover I call God as witness against my soul, that to spare you I came no more to Corinth. 24Not that we have dominion over your faith, but are fellow workers for your joy; for by faith you stand.

CHAPTER 2

A Letter Instead of a Painful Visit

1But I determined this within myself, that I would not come again to you in sorrow. 2For if I make you sorrowful, then who is he who makes me glad but the one who is made sorrowful by me?

3And I wrote this very thing to you, lest, when I came, I should have sorrow over those from whom I ought to have joy, having confidence in you all that my joy is *the joy* of you all. 4For out of much affliction and anguish of heart I wrote to you, with many tears, not that you should be grieved, but that you might know the love which I have so abundantly for you.

Forgiving a Repentant Brother

**2:5–11
see pg. 620** 5But if anyone has caused grief, he has not grieved me, but all of you to some extent—not to be too severe. 6This punishment which *was inflicted* by the majority *is* sufficient for such a man, 7so that, on the contrary, you *ought* rather to forgive and comfort *him,* lest perhaps such a one be swallowed up with too much sorrow. 8Therefore I urge you to reaffirm *your* love to him. 9For to this end I also wrote, that I might put you to the test, whether you are obedient in all things. 10Now whom you forgive anything, I also *forgive*. For if indeed I have forgiven anything, I have forgiven that one[a] for your sakes in the presence of Christ, 11lest Satan should take advantage of us; for we are not ignorant of his devices.

Christ Leads in Triumph

12Furthermore, when I came to Troas to *preach* Christ's gospel, and a door was opened to me by the Lord, 13I had no rest in my spirit, because I did not find Titus my brother; but taking my leave of them, I departed for Macedonia.

14Now thanks *be* to God who always leads us in triumph in Christ, and through us diffuses the fragrance of His knowledge in every place. 15For we

(Bible text continued on page 621)

. . . .

Affirmative Action

 **A CLOSER LOOK
1:19–20** *God doesn't equivocate in what He promises. Christ was His ultimate statement in the affirmative (vv. 19–20). Do you believe that God can be depended on to honor His word? See "Promises," Rom. 4:16–25.*

1:10 [a]NU-Text reads *shall.*   1:11 [a]M-Text reads *your behalf.*   2:10 [a]NU-Text reads *For indeed, what I have forgiven, if I have forgiven anything, I did it.*

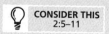

ACCOUNTABILITY

The discipline of a Corinthian believer (v. 6) points to one of the important functions of the body of Christ—to hold its members accountable for how they conduct their lives. In the case mentioned here, the censure of the church caused the offender to repent and change his ways, restoring his spiritual life and bringing joy to the church.

Accountability is easy to talk about but difficult to practice. No one likes to be judged by others. In modern society it's especially easy to feel that one's personal life is no one else's business. But a study of Scripture reveals a number of important principles about accountability:

(1) *As believers, we are accountable not only for our actions, but also for our attitudes.* In the performance-oriented work world, evaluations tend to measure results alone—higher sales, greater cost control, more clients served. Everything is quantitative. But God is interested in our innermost heart. He looks at the quality of our character. As God told Samuel, "The Lord does not see as man sees; for man looks at the outward appearance, but the Lord looks at the heart" (1 Sam. 16:7).

(2) *Accountability depends on trust.* To hold ourselves accountable to others is to to trust their judgment and to believe that they are committed to the same truths and values that we are. It also helps if we can sense that they have our best interests at heart. That's why Paul pleaded with the Corinthians to forsake their divisions and "be perfectly joined together in the same mind and in the same judgment" (1 Cor. 1:10). Without that unity, they would never submit to each other.

(3) *Accountability is directly related to the principle of submission.* Every person must struggle with the natural tendency toward rebellion against God. Accountability involves allowing others to enter into that struggle with us. But that means that sometimes we must defer to the judgment or counsel of another, es-

pecially when they challenge us with clear-cut Scriptural truth or the wisdom of personal experience. Paul told the Ephesians that part of living in the will of the Lord involves "submitting to one another in the fear of God" (Eph. 5:21).

It's not surprising that participation in the body of Christ would involve accountability, because all of us experience accountability in many other areas of life. For example, the government holds us accountable for obeying the law and paying taxes. Likewise, government officials are accountable to the public for their decisions. Employees are accountable to the boss for their work. Likewise, corporate officers are accountable to stockholders for quarterly financial results. In short, accountability touches us at home, at work, at church, and even at play.

But our attitudes toward accountability in general ultimately reflect our attitude toward accountability to God. If we are rebellious toward the One who created us and loves us most, how able will we be to submit to others? ◆

are to God the fragrance of Christ among those who are being saved and among those who are perishing. ¹⁶To the one *we are* the aroma of death *leading* to death, and to the other the aroma of life *leading* to life. And who is sufficient for these things? ¹⁷For we are not, as so many,ᵃ peddling the word of God; but as of sincerity, but as from God, we speak in the sight of God in Christ.

CHAPTER 3

Paul's Best Defense: The Corinthians Themselves

¹Do we begin again to commend ourselves? Or do we need, as some *others,* epistles of commendation to you or *letters* of commendation from you? ²You are our epistle written in our hearts, known and read by all men; ³clearly *you are* an epistle of Christ, ministered by us, written not with ink but by the Spirit of the living God, not on tablets of stone but on tablets of flesh, *that is,* of the heart.

⁴And we have such trust through Christ toward God. ⁵Not that we are sufficient of ourselves to think of anything as *being* from ourselves, but our sufficiency *is* from God,

3:6

⁶who also made us sufficient as ministers of the new covenant, not of the letter but of the Spirit;ᵃ for the letter kills, but the Spirit gives life.

2:17 ᵃM-Text reads *the rest.* 3:6 ᵃOr *spirit*

* *

The New Covenant

A CLOSER LOOK
3:6
God promised a new covenant through the prophet Jeremiah in which He would write His Law on human hearts. This suggested a new level of obedience and a new knowledge of the Lord. See "The New Covenant," 1 Cor. 11:25.

IMAGE-CONSCIOUS

CONSIDER THIS
3:7–18
When other people look at you, what do they see? What image do you project to coworkers, customers, friends, and neighbors? As Paul traveled through the cities of the Roman Empire, he always gave thought to how he would be perceived, but his biggest concern was whether observers would see Jesus in him.

To illustrate this principle, Paul recalled a phenomenon that occurred during the period in which Moses received the Law (vv. 7, 13). As Israel wandered through the wilderness, God revealed Himself to the people through what looked like a consuming fire (Ex. 24:17). But to Moses He spoke face to face (33:11). This encounter with the Living God had such an effect on Moses that his face would shine with an afterglow whenever he returned to the people. To dispel their fear, he put a veil over his face to hide the glory that resulted from his proximity to God.

Paul argues that we as believers have an even closer proximity to God than Moses did, for God Himself lives inside us (v. 8). Thus, when we meet others, they ought to see the glory of God shining out of us (vv. 9–11, 18). In other words, they ought to see Jesus.

Is that who people see when they look at us? Do they see Jesus' love, integrity, and power? Or do we "veil" the Light of the World (Matt. 5:14–16) under a mask of selfish ambition and worldly concerns?

The New Testament Ministry

3:7–18
see pg. 621

[7]But if the ministry of death, written *and* engraved on stones, was glorious, so that the children of Israel could not look steadily at the face of Moses because of the glory of his countenance, which *glory* was passing away, [8]how will the ministry of the Spirit not be more glorious? [9]For if the ministry of condemnation *had* glory, the ministry of righteousness exceeds much more in glory. [10]For even what was made glorious had no glory in this respect, because of the glory that excels. [11]For if what is passing away *was* glorious, what remains *is* much more glorious.

[12]Therefore, since we have such hope, we use great boldness of speech— [13]unlike Moses, *who* put a veil over his face so that the children of Israel could not look steadily at the end of what was passing away. [14]But their minds were blinded. For until this day the same veil remains unlifted in the reading of the Old Testament, because the *veil* is taken away in Christ. [15]But even to this day, when Moses is read, a

---

CONSIDER THIS
4:2

A CODE OF ETHICS FOR CHRISTIAN WITNESS

When believers present the message of Christ, we need to be like Paul, absolutely above board in our motives and manners (v. 2). We need to respect our hearers and refuse to do anything that would violate their integrity. Otherwise we become like a cult, peddling spiritual goods (2:17).

Here are some suggestions (from material distributed by Inter Varsity Christian Fellowship) to guide Christians in their witness:

ETHICS FOR WITNESSING
(1) We are Christians, called by God to honor Jesus Christ with our lives, abiding by biblically defined ethical standards in every area of life, public and private. This includes our efforts to persuade coworkers and others to believe the good news about Jesus Christ.
(2) Wherever we live and work, we seek to follow the mandate, motives, message, and model of Jesus, who still pursues and reclaims those lost in sin and rebelling against Him.
(3) We believe all people are created in God's image with the capacity to relate to their Creator and Redeemer. We disdain any effort to influence people which depersonalizes them or deprives them of their inherent value as persons.
(4) Since we respect the value of persons, we believe all are worthy of hearing about Jesus Christ. We also affirm the right of every person to survey other religious options. People are free to choose a different belief system than Christianity.

Continued

veil lies on their heart. ¹⁶Nevertheless when one turns to the Lord, the veil is taken away. ¹⁷Now the Lord is the Spirit; and where the Spirit of the Lord *is*, there *is* liberty. ¹⁸But we all, with unveiled face, beholding as in a mirror the glory of the Lord, are being transformed into the same image from glory to glory, just as by the Spirit of the Lord.

CHAPTER 4

Christ Is the Message

¹Therefore, since we have this ministry, as we have received mercy, we do not lose heart. ²But we have renounced the hidden things of shame, not walking in craftiness nor handling the word of God deceitfully, but by manifestation of the truth commending ourselves to every man's conscience in the sight of God. ³But even if our gospel is veiled, it is veiled to those who are perishing, ⁴whose minds the god of this age has

4:2

• • • • • • • • • • • • • • • • • •

Continued

(5) We affirm the role and right of Christians to share the gospel of Christ in the marketplace of ideas. However, this does not justify any means to fulfill that end. We reject coercive techniques or manipulative appeals, especially those that play on emotions and discount or contradict reason or evidence. We will not bypass a person's critical faculties, prey upon psychological weaknesses, undermine a relationship with one's family or religious institution, or mask the true nature of Christian conversion. We will not intentionally mislead.

(6) We respect the individual integrity, intellectual honesty, and academic freedom of others, both believers and skeptics, and so we proclaim Christ without hidden agendas. We reveal our own identity, purpose, theological positions, and sources of information. We will use no false advertising and seek no material gain from presenting the gospel.

(7) We invite people of other religious persuasions to join us in true dialogue. We acknowledge our humanness—that we Christians are just as sinful, needy, and dependent on the grace of God as anyone else. We seek to listen sensitively in order to understand, and thus rid our witness of any stereotypes or fixed formulae which block honest communication.

(8) As our "brothers' keepers," we accept our responsibility to admonish any Christian brother or sister who presents the message of Christ in a way that violates these ethical guidelines.

◆

JUST PLAIN JARS

CONSIDER THIS
4:7

As humans, we are earthen vessels— plain old clay pots (v. 7). We may drape our human frame with fancy clothes, surround it with glittering possessions, transport it in rolling splendor, or rest it on a seat of power. But in the end, we are still just human beings. Certainly we have dignity and value in God's sight, but as believers we hold something of incomparably greater value—the treasure of Christ's grace and light!

A child picks a fragrant bouquet of wildflowers for her mother and places them in an old mayonnaise jar for a vase. What does the mother pay attention to? What delights her heart? The flowers or the mayonnaise jar?

Our value as vessels lies in the incomparable beauty and splendor of what we hold, not in our shape or color.

blinded, who do not believe, lest the light of the gospel of the glory of Christ, who is the image of God, should shine on them. [5]For we do not preach ourselves, but Christ Jesus the Lord, and ourselves your bondservants for Jesus' sake. [6]For it is the God who commanded light to shine out of darkness, who has shone in our hearts to *give* the light of the knowledge of the glory of God in the face of Jesus Christ.

Natural Messengers, Supernatural Power

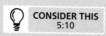

4:7
see pg. 623

[7]But we have this treasure in earthen vessels, that the excellence of the power may be of God and not of us. [8]*We are* hard-pressed on every side, yet not crushed; *we are* perplexed, but not in despair; [9]persecuted, but not forsaken; struck down, but not destroyed— [10]always carrying about in the body the dying of the Lord Jesus, that the life of Jesus also may be manifested in our body. [11]For we who live are always delivered to death for Jesus' sake, that the life of Jesus also may be manifested in our mortal flesh. [12]So then death is working in us, but life in you.

[13]And since we have the same spirit of faith, according to what is written, "I believed and therefore I spoke,"[a] we also believe and therefore speak, [14]knowing that He who raised up the Lord Jesus will also raise us up with Jesus, and will

4:13 [a]Psalm 116:10

CONSIDER THIS
5:10

THE JUDGMENT SEAT

Have you ever felt wronged and had someone say, "Don't worry, you'll have your day in court"? All of us will eventually have our "day in court" before God when we stand before the judgment seat (bēma) of Christ (v. 10).

Paul's Corinthian readers must have been quite familiar with the bēma. As in most cities of Greece, a large, richly decorated rostrum called the bēma stood in the middle of the marketplace at Corinth. It was used by the officials for purposes of public proclamations, commendations, and condemnations.

Paul himself had been brought to the Corinthian bēma by Jews who opposed his message. The case was heard by Gallio, the Roman proconsul (governor) of the region, who dismissed the complaint (Acts 18:12–17).

But the bēma was used for more than just tribunals. It was at the bēma that winners of Corinth's prestigious athletic contests were announced (see "The Games," 1 Cor. 9:24–27). Thus, Paul's statement that believers will appear

present *us* with you. ¹⁵For all things *are* for your sakes, that grace, having spread through the many, may cause thanksgiving to abound to the glory of God.

¹⁶Therefore we do not lose heart. Even though our outward man is perishing, yet the inward *man* is being renewed day by day. ¹⁷For our light affliction, which is but for a moment, is working for us a far more exceeding *and* eternal weight of glory, ¹⁸while we do not look at the things which are seen, but at the things which are not seen. For the things which are seen *are* temporary, but the things which are not seen *are* eternal.

CHAPTER 5

We Are Headed for Eternity with God

¹For we know that if our earthly house, *this* tent, is destroyed, we have a building from God, a house not made with hands, eternal in the heavens. ²For

> 🔅 **5:2–5**

in this we groan, earnestly desiring to be clothed with our habitation which is from heaven, ³if indeed, having been clothed, we shall not be found naked. ⁴For we who are in *this* tent groan, being burdened, not because we want to be unclothed, but further clothed, that mortality may be swallowed up by life. ⁵Now He who has prepared us for this very thing *is* God, who also has given us the Spirit as a guarantee.

* * * * * * * * * * * * * * * * * * * *

before the bēma *of Christ is as much a cause for joy and hope as it is for fear.*

One thing is certain: the judgment rendered at the bēma *will be fair, for Christ will be the Judge, and He Himself once stood before Pilate's* bēma *(Matt. 27:19; John 19:10). He knows what it feels like to have one's life weighed in the balance.*

However, the Lord will not be deciding the eternal fate of believers as He sits on His bēma; *that was settled at the moment of salvation (John 5:24). Instead, the* bēma *of Christ will be our chance as believers to look at our lives according to Christ's perfect assessment. It will be the ultimate opportunity to experience honest evaluation and true justice as we stand before Him.*

What will Christ say of you? Are you paying attention to your "deeds done in the body" in light of this moment of accountability? Are you striving to earn the Lord's praise in every area of life? ◆

WHAT DID YOU EXPECT?

> 🔅 **CONSIDER THIS**
> **5:2-5**

In much of the world, evil abounds and Christians suffer. Yet many Western believers assume that health and wealth ought to be the norm. It's not just that they hope for these—they *expect* them, as if God somehow owes them prosperity in exchange for their faith or integrity or some other Christian virtue.

What a far cry from Paul's day, when "groaning" was the normal experience of people, believers and unbelievers alike (vv. 2, 4). Certainly Paul exulted in the "new creation" that God brings about (5:17). But having celebrated that marvelous reality, Paul went on to say that life in Christ involves troubles and pain (6:4–10). Only from our glorified bodies will God remove all suffering (5:1).

What does this say to modern Christians in the West? We may enjoy health, wealth, and success, but isn't that the exception rather than the rule, at least judging by the experience of believers throughout history and around the world today? How much do we really know about *normal* Christianity?

Paul directly attacked the idea that God rewards godliness with material blessing. See "The Dangers of Prosperity Theology," 1 Tim. 6:3–6.

6So *we are* always confident, knowing that while we are at
home in the body we are absent from the Lord. 7For we
walk by faith, not by sight. 8We are confident, yes, well
pleased rather to be absent from the body and to be present
with the Lord.

9Therefore we make it our aim, whether present or ab-

5:10
see pg. 624

sent, to be well pleasing to Him. 10For we
must all appear before the judgment seat
of Christ, that each one may receive the things *done* in the
body, according to what he has done, whether good or bad.
11Knowing, therefore, the terror of the Lord, we persuade
men; but we are well known to God, and I also trust are
well known in your consciences.

A New Creation in Christ

12For we do not commend ourselves again to you, but
give you opportunity to boast on our behalf, that you may
have *an answer* for those who boast in appearance and not
in heart. 13For if we are beside ourselves, *it is* for God; or if
we are of sound mind, *it is* for you. 14For the love of Christ
compels us, because we judge thus: that if One died for all,

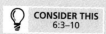

CONSIDER THIS
6:3–10

Welcome to Stressful Living

For many people in the world today, tension, conflict, weariness, and suffering have become commonplace. Nevertheless, some offer the vain hope that life's troubles can be done away with, that we can somehow get to the point where things will always be great. They suggest that faith in Christ will deliver us into a state of serenity and ease and bring prosperity, health, and constant pleasure.

However, that was neither the experience nor the teaching of early Christians such as Paul, James, or Peter, and certainly not of their Lord Jesus. Paul described the life of a servant of God in terms of tribulation, distress, tumult, and sleeplessness (vv. 4–5). But he also linked these stress producers with rich treasures that money cannot buy: purity, kindness, sincere love, honor, good report, joy, and the possession of all things (vv. 6–10).

So as long as we live as God's people on this earth, we can expect a connection between trouble and hope. That connection is never pleasant, but our troubles can bring about lasting benefits:

> Jesus *told us that if we want to follow Him, we must deny ourselves and take up a cross. If we try to save our lives, we will only lose them. But if we lose our lives for His sake, we will find them (Matt. 16:24–25).*

then all died; ¹⁵and He died for all, that those who live should live no longer for themselves, but for Him who died for them and rose again.

¹⁶Therefore, from now on, we regard no one according to the flesh. Even though we have known Christ according to 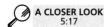 the flesh, yet now we know *Him thus* no longer. ¹⁷Therefore, if anyone *is* in Christ, *he is* a new creation; old things have passed away; behold, all things have become new. ¹⁸Now all things *are* of God, who has reconciled us to Himself through Jesus Christ, and has given us the ministry of reconciliation, ¹⁹that is, that God was in Christ reconciling the world to Himself, not imputing their trespasses to them, and has committed to us the word of reconciliation.

²⁰Now then, we are ambassadors for Christ, as though

A New Creation

A CLOSER LOOK
5:17
In what sense do we become "a new creation" in Christ (v. 17)? Paul painted several pictures of what that looks like. See "New Creatures with New Character," Gal. 5:22–23.

The writer to the Hebrews encouraged us that our troubles are often a sign that we are legitimate children of God, who lovingly disciplines us to train us in righteousness (Heb. 12:8–11).

James encouraged us to rejoice in our various trials, because as they test our faith, they produce patience, which ultimately makes us mature in Christ (James 1:2–4).

Peter knew by personal experience the kind of pressure that can cause one's allegiance to Christ to waiver. He warned us that "fiery trials" are nothing strange, but that they actually allow us to experience something of Christ's sufferings so that we can ultimately experience something of His glory, too (1 Pet. 4:12–13).

We can count on feeling stress if we're going to obey Christ. But we can take hope! That stress is preparing us for riches we will enjoy for eternity. ◆

OLD **THINGS HAVE PASSED AWAY; BEHOLD, ALL THINGS HAVE BECOME NEW.**
—2 Corinthians 5:17

God were pleading through us: we implore *you* on Christ's behalf, be reconciled to God. 21For He made Him who knew no sin *to be* sin for us, that we might become the righteousness of God in Him.

CHAPTER 6

Openness and Authenticity

1We then, *as* workers together *with Him* also plead with *you* not to receive the grace of God in vain. 2For He says:

"In an acceptable time I have heard you,
And in the day of salvation I have helped you."*a*

Behold, now *is* the accepted time; behold, now *is* the day of salvation.

6:3–10 see pg. 626 3We give no offense in anything, that our ministry may not be blamed. 4But in all *things* we commend ourselves as ministers of God: in much patience, in tribulations, in needs, in distresses, 5in stripes, in imprisonments, in tumults, in labors, in sleeplessness, in fastings; 6by purity, by knowledge, by longsuffering, by kindness, by the Holy Spirit, by sincere love, 7by the word of truth, by the power of God, by the armor of righteousness on the right hand and on the left, 8by honor and dishonor, by evil report and good report; as deceivers, and *yet* true; 9as unknown, and *yet* well known; as dying, and behold we live; as chastened, and *yet* not killed; 10as sorrowful, yet always rejoicing; as poor, yet making many rich; as having nothing, and *yet* possessing all things.

11O Corinthians! We have spoken openly to you, our heart is wide open. 12You are not restricted by us, but you are restricted by your *own* affections. 13Now in return for the same (I speak as to children), you also be open.

Avoid Immoral Partnerships

14Do not be unequally yoked together with unbelievers. For what fellowship has righteousness with lawlessness? And what communion has light with darkness? 15And what accord has Christ with Belial? Or what part has a believer with an unbeliever? 16And what agreement has the temple of God with idols? For you*a* are the temple of the living God. As God has said:

"I will dwell in them
And walk among *them.*
I will be their God,
And they shall be My people."*b*

17Therefore

"Come out from among them
And be separate, says the Lord.
Do not touch what is unclean,
And I will receive you."*a*
18 "I will be a Father to you,
And you shall be My sons and daughters,
Says the Lord Almighty."*a*

CHAPTER 7

1Therefore, having these promises, beloved, let us cleanse ourselves from all filthiness of the flesh and spirit, perfecting holiness in the fear of God.

Be Open toward Each Other

2Open *your hearts* to us. We have wronged no one, we have corrupted no one, we have cheated no one. 3I do not say *this* to condemn; for I have said before that you are in our hearts, to die together and to live together. 4Great *is* my boldness of speech toward you, great *is* my boasting on your behalf. I am filled with comfort. I am exceedingly joyful in all our tribulation.

5For indeed, when we came to Macedonia, our bodies had no rest, but we were troubled on every side. Outside *were* conflicts, inside *were* fears.

✓ 7:6 6Nevertheless God, who comforts the downcast, comforted us by the coming of Titus, 7and not only by his coming, but also by the consolation with which he was comforted in you, when he told us of your earnest desire, your mourning, your zeal for me, so that I rejoiced even more.

8For even if I made you sorry with my letter, I do not regret it; though I did regret it. For I perceive that the same epistle made you sorry, though only for a while. 9Now I rejoice, not that you were made sorry, but that your sorrow led to repentance. For you were made sorry in a godly manner, that you might suffer loss from us in nothing. 10For godly

6:2 *a*Isaiah 49:8   6:16 *a*NU-Text reads *we.*   *b*Leviticus 26:12; Jeremiah 32:38; Ezekiel 37:27   6:17 *a*Isaiah 52:11; Ezekiel 20:34, 41   6:18 *a*2 Samuel 7:14

sorrow produces repentance *leading* to salvation, not to be regretted; but the sorrow of the world produces death. ¹¹For observe this very thing, that you sorrowed in a godly manner: What diligence it produced in you, *what* clearing *of yourselves, what* indignation, *what* fear, *what* vehement desire, *what* zeal, *what* vindication! In all *things* you proved yourselves to be clear in this matter. ¹²Therefore, although I wrote to you, *I did* not *do it* for the sake of him who had done the wrong, nor for the sake of him who suffered wrong, but that our care for you in the sight of God might appear to you.

¹³Therefore we have been comforted in your comfort. And we rejoiced exceedingly more for the joy of Titus, because his spirit has been refreshed by you all. ¹⁴For if in anything I have boasted to him about you, I am not ashamed. But as we spoke all things to you in truth, even so our boasting to Titus was found true. ¹⁵And his affections are greater for you as he remembers the obedience of you all, how with fear and trembling you received him. ¹⁶Therefore I rejoice that I have confidence in you in everything.

CHAPTER 8

The Example of the Macedonians

¹Moreover, brethren, we make known to you the grace of God bestowed on the churches of Macedonia: ²that in a

THE MAN OF THE HOUR

Titus was a man for tough tasks. According to Paul, he was dependable (2 Cor. 8:17), reliable (7:6), and diligent (8:17). He also had a great capacity for human affection (7:13–15). Tradition holds that he was the first bishop of Crete. Possessing both strength and tact, Titus calmed a desperate situation on more than one occasion. He serves as a good model for believers living under trying circumstances.

Titus' ethnic background proved to be important and useful to the early church. As an uncircumcised Gentile, he accompanied Paul and Barnabas to Jerusalem, where many of the Jewish Christians were debating whether non-Jews could be saved. Paul introduced him there as a living example of a great theological truth—that Gentiles need not be circumcised (that is, become Jews) in order to receive the grace of God (Gal. 2:1–3).

PERSONALITY PROFILE: TITUS

 FOR YOUR INFO 7:6 **Not to be confused with:** The Roman general Titus who destroyed Jerusalem in A.D. 70 (see "Jerusalem Surrounded," Luke 21:20).

Background: Raised as a Greek-speaking Gentile.

Known for: Diplomacy, public relations, project management, and fund-raising. Paul praised him as dependable, reliable, and diligent.

Best known today for: His work with Paul as a traveling companion and coworker in establishing churches throughout the Roman world.

Does it really matter what you believe, as long as you do the right thing? Yes it does, thought Paul. That's why he wrote to Titus, his valued associate on Crete, urging him to teach "sound doctrine." He knew that correct living is a product of correct belief. To learn more about the situation, see the Introduction to Titus.

great trial of affliction the abundance of their joy and their deep poverty abounded in the riches of their liberality. ³For I bear witness that according to *their* ability, yes, and beyond *their* ability, *they were* freely willing, ⁴imploring us with much urgency that we would receiveᵃ the gift and the fellowship of the ministering to the saints. ⁵And not *only* as we had hoped, but they first gave themselves to the Lord, and *then* to us by the will of God. ⁶So we urged Titus, that as he had begun, so he would also complete this grace in you as well. ⁷But as you abound in everything—in faith, in speech, in knowledge, in all diligence, and in your love for us—*see* that you abound in this grace also.

The Example of Christ

 8:8–9

⁸I speak not by commandment, but I am testing the sincerity of your love by

8:4 ᵃNU-Text and M-Text omit *that we would receive*, thus changing text to *urgency for the favor and fellowship . . . .*

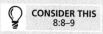 CONSIDER THIS
8:8–9

CHRIST BECAME POOR

Almost anyone can "love" people in the abstract. But when it comes time to express that love—by lending a helping hand or writing a check—one can quickly determine the sincerity of a person's love for others. That was Paul's point in vv. 8–9. To illustrate it, he used the ultimate model of tangible love—Jesus Christ.

Christ became poor in order to make us rich. Consider what He gave up when He left heaven and took on a human body:

- He left His Father, whose immediate presence He would not enjoy again for more than 30 years. How long would you be willing to be away from your closest companion and friend in order to help a group of people—especially if you knew that most of them would reject and despise you, and might even kill you?
- We can imagine that He left a joyful crowd that included Abraham, Isaac, Jacob, the angelic hosts, and all the redeemed saints who were worshiping Him, glorifying Him, and having fellowship with Him prior to His incarnation. He left those who loved Him to come and be misunderstood, rejected, scorned, hated, and scourged by most of those He came to help. Would you leave a position of honor and adoration to go help people who would by and large reject you?
- He left a heavenly home that far exceeded in splendor, majesty, and comfort the physical environment of His

the diligence of others. ⁹For you know the grace of our Lord Jesus Christ, that though He was rich, yet for your sakes He became poor, that you through His poverty might become rich.

¹⁰And in this I give advice: It is to your advantage not only to be doing what you began and were desiring to do a year ago; ¹¹but now you also must complete the doing *of it;* that as *there was* a readiness to desire *it,* so *there* also *may be* a completion out of what *you* have. ¹²For if there is first a willing mind, *it is* accepted according to what one has, *and* not according to what he does not have.

 8:13–15 ¹³For *I do* not *mean* that others should be eased and you burdened; ¹⁴but by an equality, *that* now at this time your abundance *may supply* their lack, that their abundance also may supply your lack—that there may be equality. ¹⁵As it is written, "He who *gathered* much had nothing left over, and he who *gathered* little had no lack."ᵃ

8:15 ᵃExodus 16:18

♦ ♦ ♦ ♦ ♦ ♦ ♦ ♦ ♦ ♦ ♦ ♦

earthly life. Would you give up the best accommodations this earth has to offer in order to help needy people in a bad neighborhood?

• He left His pre-incarnate existence in the form of God, without limitations, to take on a physical body subject to fatigue, aches, and pains. Would you accept hunger, thirst, fatigue, pain, and limited physical abilities to help people who didn't even care whether you came or not?

The statement that Christ became poor puts into perspective Jesus' command to the rich young ruler to sell what he had and give the proceeds to the poor (Mark 10:21), and His instruction to the disciples to sell what they had and give alms, providing themselves treasure in heaven (Luke 12:33). What Jesus asked them to do, He had already done—to such a degree, in fact, that their obedience could never equal His selflessness. ◆

SOLIDARITY

CONSIDER THIS
8:13–15 Paul challenged the Corinthian Christians to participate in a fund-raising project to benefit believers at Jerusalem. But he seemed to be concerned with more than money. He wanted Gentile churches like Corinth to start practicing solidarity with their Jewish brothers and sisters (vv. 13–15, 24). It's almost as if the new churches owed something, in a sense, to the original church in Jerusalem.

Jesus worked as a carpenter and lived responsibly. But the fact remains, He was born poor and lived poor. In fact, He was homeless. See Matt. 8:20.

Christ may have been poor, but many of His followers today are not. How should wealthy believers handle their money? See "Christians and Money," 1 Tim. 6:6–19.

REAPING THE BENEFITS

💡 **CONSIDER THIS**
9:6-8

Paul wanted the Corinthians to give generously toward a fund-raising project to help needy Christians. He linked generosity with spiritual benefits: the more one gives, the more one benefits (vv. 6–11).

This principle goes beyond financial giving. At work, for example, you may donate toward the local United Way. But when a coworker asks for some of your time to talk about a problem, what is your response? Do you give your attention generously or grudgingly? When your boss gives you a special assignment, do you give the project just enough attention to get it over with, or do you jump in wholeheartedly with energy and creativity?

What about your time and emotional energy after hours? When your spouse or children need you, do you make yourself available generously or grudgingly? Do you give a fair contribution of yourself to assignments that you've volunteered for, or just a token effort?

We are constant recipients of God's generous grace. He promises that if we will give of ourselves, He'll enable us to have an abundance of resources for the work to which He has called us (v. 8).

Giving generously in order to gain spiritual benefits does not mean that God rewards godliness with material blessings. See "The Dangers of Prosperity Theology," 1 Tim. 6:3–6.

A Plan to Provide Material Help

[16]But thanks *be* to God who puts[a] the same earnest care for you into the heart of Titus. [17]For he not only accepted the exhortation, but being more diligent, he went to you of his own accord. [18]And we have sent with him the brother whose praise *is* in the gospel throughout all the churches, [19]and not only *that,* but who was also chosen by the churches to travel with us with this gift, which is administered by us to the glory of the Lord Himself and *to show* your ready mind, [20]avoiding this: that anyone should blame us in this lavish gift which is administered by us— [21]providing honorable things, not only in the sight of the Lord, but also in the sight of men.

[22]And we have sent with them our brother whom we have often proved diligent in many things, but now much more diligent, because of the great confidence which *we* have in you. [23]If *anyone inquires* about Titus, *he is* my partner and fellow worker concerning you. Or if our brethren *are inquired about, they are* messengers of the churches, the glory of Christ. [24]Therefore show to them, and[a] before the churches the proof of your love and of our boasting on your behalf.

CHAPTER 9

Implementing the Plan

[1]Now concerning the ministering to the saints, it is superfluous for me to write to you; [2]for I know your willingness, about which I boast of you to the Macedonians, that Achaia was ready a year ago; and your zeal has stirred up the majority. [3]Yet I have sent the brethren, lest our boasting of you should be in vain in this respect, that, as I said, you may be ready; [4]lest if *some* Macedonians come with me and find you unprepared, we (not to mention you!) should be ashamed of this confident boasting.[a] [5]Therefore I thought it necessary to exhort the brethren to go to you ahead of time, and prepare your generous gift beforehand, which *you had* previously promised, that it may be ready as *a matter of* generosity and not as a grudging obligation.

The Blessings of Generosity

💡 **9:6-8**

[6]But this *I* say: He who sows sparingly will also reap sparingly, and he who sows bountifully will also reap bountifully. [7]So let each one *give* as he purposes in his heart, not grudgingly or of necessity; for God loves a cheerful giver. [8]And God *is* able to make all grace abound toward you, that you, always having all suffi-

8:16 [a]NU-Text reads *has put.*   8:24 [a]NU-Text and M-Text omit *and.*   9:4 [a]NU-Text reads *this confidence.*

ciency in all *things,* may have an abundance for every good

9:9–10 work. ⁹As it is written:

> "He has dispersed abroad,
> He has given to the poor;
> His righteousness endures forever."*a*

¹⁰Now may*a* He who supplies seed to the sower, and bread for food, supply and multiply the seed you have *sown* and increase the fruits of your righteousness, ¹¹while *you are* enriched in everything for all liberality, which causes thanksgiving through us to God. ¹²For the administration of this service not only supplies the needs of the saints, but also is abounding through many thanksgivings to God, ¹³while, through the proof of this ministry, they glorify God for the obedience of your confession to the gospel of Christ, and for *your* liberal sharing with them and all *men,* ¹⁴and by their prayer for you, who long for you because of the exceeding grace of God in you. ¹⁵Thanks *be* to God for His indescribable gift!

CHAPTER 10

An Appeal for Obedience

10:1
see pg. 634   ¹Now I, Paul, myself am pleading with you by the meekness and gentleness of Christ—who in presence *am* lowly among you, but being absent am bold toward you. ²But I beg *you* that when I am present I may not be bold with that confidence by which I intend to be bold against some, who think of us as if we walked according to the flesh. ³For though we walk in the flesh, we do not war according to the flesh. ⁴For the weapons of our warfare *are* not carnal but mighty in God for pulling down strongholds, ⁵casting down arguments and every high thing that exalts itself against the knowledge of God, bringing every thought into captivity to the obedience of Christ, ⁶and being ready to punish all disobedience when your obedience is fulfilled.

Paul Defends His Personal Integrity

⁷Do you look at things according to the outward appearance? If anyone is convinced in himself that he is Christ's, let him again consider this in himself, that just as he *is* Christ's, even so we *are* Christ's.*a* ⁸For even if I should boast somewhat more about our authority, which the Lord gave us*a* for edification and not for your destruction, I shall not be ashamed— ⁹lest I seem to terrify you by letters. ¹⁰"For

9:9 *a*Psalm 112:9   9:10 *a*NU-Text reads *Now He who supplies . . . will supply. . . .*
10:7 *a*NU-Text reads *even as we are.*   10:8 *a*NU-Text omits *us.*

WHO ARE THE POOR?

CONSIDER THIS
9:9–10   **By comparison to the many modern Christians who live in affluence, the Corinthian believers would appear poor. Yet Paul described the Christians of Macedonia as living in "deep poverty" (8:2), so they were much poorer even than the Corinthians. What does Scripture mean, then, when it says that God "has given to *the poor*" (9:9, italics added)? And what does that mean for believers today who are relatively affluent?**

The word for *poor* (v. 9) described someone who toiled for a living, what we would call a day laborer. Such persons were distinct from the truly destitute. The former may have had a difficult life, but at least they were in no danger of losing it. By contrast, the truly poor were in immediate danger of perishing if they didn't receive charitable aid.

Paul described God as dispersing to the *poor,* the day laborers, not food for survival but seed that they could sow to raise a crop (vv. 9–10). He indicated that God would aid the Corinthians so that they, in turn, could aid the completely destitute believers in Jerusalem.

So what does that mean for us as Christians today if we work at relatively stable, well-paid jobs, own our own homes, and manage to salt away at least some money for retirement? Paul would doubtless identify us as rich. We may work hard, but we have disposable income that most first-century Christians could have only imagined.

his letters," they say, "*are* weighty and powerful, but *his* bodily presence *is* weak, and *his* speech contemptible." [11]Let such a person consider this, that what we are in word by letters when we are absent, such *we will* also *be* in deed when we are present.

[12]For we dare not class ourselves or compare ourselves with those who commend themselves. But they, measuring themselves by themselves, and comparing themselves among themselves, are not wise. [13]We, however, will not boast beyond measure, but within the limits of the sphere which God appointed us—a sphere which especially includes you. [14]For we are not overextending ourselves (as though *our authority* did not extend to you), for it was to you that we came with the gospel of Christ; [15]not boasting of things beyond measure, *that is,* in other men's labors, but having hope, *that* as your faith is increased, we shall be greatly enlarged by you in our sphere, [16]to preach the gospel in the *regions* beyond you, *and* not to boast in another man's sphere of accomplishment.

[17]But "he who glories, let him glory in the LORD."[a] [18]For

10:17 [a]Jeremiah 9:24

CONSIDER THIS
10:1

INTEGRITY IN THE FACE OF COMPETITION

When you face a competitive situation, are you tempted to do whatever *it* takes to win? Paul faced severe competition at Corinth. In chapters 10–12, he described real danger to his work in Corinth:

- Opposing leaders and teachers were making headway. Paul's people were tempted to cross over to them (10:15; 11:3–4, 12–15).
- Paul felt the pain of this loss very deeply (10:2–3; 11:2–3, 29).
- He felt threatened (10:8–11, 13–15; 11:5–6, 16–21).
- He loved the Corinthians and feared losing them so much that he became angry (11:11–15).
- He defended himself as a faithful servant who had suffered for the Corinthians and the gospel (10:13–18; 11:20–30; 12:11).

As Paul wrestled with mixed feelings and sketchy information, he dealt in known principles of godliness and clear communication:

- Paul was passionate about the problem. He wrote to the Corinthians extensively (see the Introduction to 1 and 2 Corinthians).

not he who commends himself is approved, but whom the Lord commends.

CHAPTER 11

Paul Defends His Apostleship

¹Oh, that you would bear with me in a little folly—and indeed you do bear with me. ²For I am jealous for you with godly jealousy. For I have betrothed you to one husband, that I may present *you as* a chaste virgin to Christ. ³But I fear, lest somehow, as the serpent deceived Eve by his craftiness, so your minds may be corrupted from the simplicity*a* that is in Christ. ⁴For if he who comes preaches another Jesus whom we have not preached, or *if* you receive a different spirit which you have not received, or a different gospel which you have not accepted—you may well put up with it!

☑ **11:5** ⁵For I consider that I am not at all inferior to the most eminent apostles. ⁶Even though *I am* untrained in speech, yet *I am* not in knowl-

11:3 *a*NU-Text adds *and purity.*

• ◆ • ◆ • ◆ • ◆ • ◆ • ◆ • ◆ • ◆ •

- *He tried to visit Corinth to discuss matters openly (10:2, 11; 12:14; 13:1).*
- *He encouraged the Corinthians to test his prior works among them if they questioned his loyalty and integrity (10:13, 15; 11:22–27). It's interesting that he felt awkward in this self-defense (11:21, 23; 12:7–10).*
- *He gave a clear statement of the finances involved in his previous work in Corinth (11:7–9; 1 Cor. 16:1–4, 16).*
- *He appealed for negotiations in a way that would honor Christ and not duplicate the world's methods (2 Cor. 10:3–4; 13:8–10).*
- *He urged in-depth analysis of the situation (10:7; 13:1, 5, 8).*

Paul faced a real temptation to resort to any means not to lose his converts in Corinth. As readers we can feel the tension in these letters. But Paul waged spiritual warfare within himself first so that he could rise above vicious, underhanded solutions. He kept the big picture, avoiding short term gains in order to live with long-term, Christlike values. ◆

WHO WERE THE APOSTLES?

☑ **FOR YOUR INFO 11:5** Paul was counted among a group of early church leaders known as "apostles" (v. 5). Each apostle was chosen by Jesus and given authority to carry out certain tasks, especially the task of making disciples of "all the nations" (Matt. 28:19).

The word *apostle* means "messenger." The term was first used of the twelve disciples whom Jesus sent out, two by two, into Galilee to expand His ministry of preaching and healing (Mark 3:14; 6:30). These same disciples, with the exception of Judas Iscariot, were recommissioned as apostles after Jesus' resurrection to be His witnesses throughout the world (Acts 1:8). After Jesus' ascension, the group brought their number to twelve again by choosing Matthias (1:23–26).

However, the term apostle came to apply to others besides the Twelve. It included people like Paul who had seen the risen Christ and were specially commissioned by Him (1 Cor. 15:10). James, the Lord's brother, was counted as an apostle (Gal. 1:19; see profile at the Introduction to James). And when Paul wrote that Jesus was seen not only by James but also by "all the apostles" (1 Cor. 15:7), he seemed to be describing a wider group than the Twelve to whom Jesus appeared earlier (1 Cor. 15:5).

The authority committed to the apostles by Christ was unique and foundational (1 Cor. 12:28; Eph. 4:11). The apostles could install elders or other leaders and teachers in the churches, and they could authorize believers to assume special responsibilities.

edge. But we have been thoroughly manifested*a* among you in all things.

[7]Did I commit sin in humbling myself that you might be exalted, because I preached the gospel of God to you free of charge? [8]I robbed other churches, taking wages *from them* to minister to you. [9]And when I was present with you, and in need, I was a burden to no one, for what I lacked the brethren who came from Macedonia supplied. And in everything I kept myself from being burdensome to you, and so I will keep *myself.* [10]As the truth of Christ is in me, no one shall stop me from this boasting in the regions of Achaia. [11]Why? Because I do not love you? God knows!

[12]But what I do, I will also continue to do, that I may cut off the opportunity from those who desire an opportunity to be regarded just as we are in the things of which they boast. [13]For such *are* false apostles, deceitful workers, transforming themselves into apostles of Christ. [14]And no wonder! For Satan himself transforms himself into an angel of light. [15]Therefore *it is* no great thing if his ministers also transform themselves into ministers of righteousness, whose end will be according to their works.

Paul's Impeccable Credentials

[16]I say again, let no one think me a fool. If otherwise, at least receive me as a fool, that I also may boast a little. [17]What I speak, I speak not according to the Lord, but as it were, foolishly, in this confidence of boasting. [18]Seeing that many boast according to the flesh, I also will boast. [19]For you put up with fools gladly, since you *yourselves* are wise! [20]For you put up with it if one brings you into bondage, if one devours *you,* if one takes *from you,* if one exalts himself, if one strikes you on the face. [21]To *our* shame I say that we were too weak for that! But in whatever anyone is bold—I speak foolishly—I am bold also.

[22]Are they Hebrews? So *am* I. Are they Israelites? So *am* I. Are they the seed of Abraham? So *am* I. [23]Are they ministers of Christ?—I speak as a fool— I *am* more: in labors more abundant, in stripes above measure, in prisons more frequently, in deaths often. [24]From the Jews five times I received forty *stripes* minus one. [25]Three times I was beaten with rods; once I was stoned; three times I was shipwrecked; a night and a day I have been in the deep; [26]in journeys often, *in* perils of waters, *in* perils of robbers, *in* perils of *my own* countrymen, *in* perils of the Gentiles, *in* perils in the city, *in* perils in the wilderness, *in* perils in the sea, *in* perils among false brethren; [27]in weariness and toil, in sleeplessness often, in hunger and thirst, in fastings often, in cold and nakedness— [28]besides the other things, what comes upon me daily: my deep concern for all the churches. [29]Who is weak, and I am not weak? Who is made to stumble, and I do not burn *with indignation?*

[30]If I must boast, I will boast in the things which concern my infirmity. [31]The God and Father of our Lord Jesus Christ, who is blessed forever, knows that I am not lying. [32]In Damascus the governor, under Aretas the king, was guarding the city of the Damascenes with a garrison, desiring to arrest me; [33]but I was let down in a basket through a window in the wall, and escaped from his hands.

CHAPTER 12

A Revelation from the Lord

[1]It is doubtless*a* not profitable for me to boast. I will come to visions and revelations of the Lord: [2]I know a man in Christ who fourteen years ago— whether in the body I do not know, or whether out of the body I do not know, God knows—such a one was caught up to the third heaven. [3]And I know such a man—whether in the body or out of the body I do not know, God knows— [4]how he was caught up into Paradise and heard inexpressible words, which it is not lawful for a man to utter. [5]Of such a one I will boast; yet of myself I will not boast, except in my infirmities. [6]For though I might desire to boast, I will not be a fool; for I will speak the truth. But I refrain, lest anyone should think of me above what he sees me *to be* or hears from me.

💡 **12:7–10** [7]And lest I should be exalted above measure by the abundance of the revelations, a thorn in the flesh was given to me, a messenger of Satan to buffet me, lest I be exalted above measure. [8]Concerning this thing I pleaded with the Lord three times that it might depart from me. [9]And He said to me, "My grace is sufficient for you, for My strength is made perfect

11:6 aNU-Text omits been. 12:1 aNU-Text reads necessary, though not profitable, to boast.

in weakness." Therefore most gladly I will rather boast in my infirmities, that the power of Christ may rest upon me. [10]Therefore I take pleasure in infirmities, in reproaches, in needs, in persecutions, in distresses, for Christ's sake. For when I am weak, then I am strong.

[11]I have become a fool in boasting;[a] you have compelled me. For I ought to have been commended by you; for in nothing was I behind the most eminent apostles, though I am nothing. [12]Truly the signs of an apostle were accomplished among you with all perseverance, in signs and wonders and mighty deeds. [13]For what is it in which you were inferior to other churches, except that I myself was not burdensome to you? Forgive me this wrong!

Paul Says He Will Visit

[14]Now *for* the third time I am ready to come to you. And I will not be burdensome to you; for I do not seek yours, but you. For the children ought not to lay up for the parents, but the parents for the children. [15]And I will very gladly spend and be spent for your souls; though the more abundantly I love you, the less I am loved.

[16]But be that *as it may*, I did not burden you. Nevertheless, being crafty, I caught you by cunning! [17]Did I take advantage of you by any of those whom I sent to you? [18]I urged Titus, and sent our brother with *him*. Did Titus take advantage of you? Did we not walk in the same spirit? Did *we* not *walk* in the same steps?

[19]Again, do you think[a] that we excuse ourselves to you? We speak before God in Christ. But *we do* all things, beloved, for your edification. [20]For I fear lest, when I come, I shall not find you such as I wish, and *that* I shall be found by you such as you do not wish; lest *there be* contentions, jealousies, outbursts of wrath, selfish ambitions, backbitings, whisperings, conceits, tumults; [21]lest, when I come again, my God will humble me among you, and I shall mourn for many who have sinned before and have not repented of the uncleanness, fornication, and lewdness which they have practiced.

CHAPTER 13

Paul Challenges the Corinthians to Prepare

[1]This *will be* the third *time* I am coming to you. "By the mouth of two or three witnesses every word shall be established."[a] [2]I have told you before, and foretell as if I were present the second time, and now being absent I write[a] to those who have sinned before, and to all the rest, that if I

WHEN I AM WEAK, THEN I AM STRONG

CONSIDER THIS 12:7–10 **Our world prizes strength—the physical strength of athletes, the financial strength of companies, the political strength of office-holders, and the military strength of armies. But Paul put a new twist on the notion of strength: weakness can make a person strong (vv. 7–10).**

Most of us would have no problem with God using our natural areas of strength, such as speaking, organizing, managing, or selling. But suppose He chose instead to use us in areas where we are weak? Moses claimed to be a poor speaker (Ex. 4:10), yet God used him as His spokesman on Israel's behalf. Peter tended to be impulsive and even hotheaded, yet God used him as one of the chief architects of the early church.

Weakness has a way of making us rely on God far more than our strengths do. What weakness in your life might God desire to use for His purposes?

12:11 [a]NU-Text omits *in boasting.*   12:19 [a]NU-Text reads *You have been thinking for a long time.* . . .   13:1 [a]Deuteronomy 19:15   13:2 [a]NU-Text omits *I write.*

SPIRITUAL AUTHORITY

💡 **CONSIDER THIS**
13:10

If you exercise leadership among other believers, you'll want to carefully study Paul's comment about his authority (v. 10). Like many of us, Paul liked to be in charge, and he felt frustrated when people failed to follow his lead, as the Corinthians had. As an apostle, he had spiritual authority over them, which at times led him to deal severely with them (1 Cor. 4:21; 5:5; compare Titus 1:13).

But it's important to notice how Paul exercised his authority, especially as he grew older in the faith. He didn't lord it over others or try to use his authority to personal advantage. Nor did he abuse his power by using it to work out his own anger. Instead, he recognized that spiritual authority is given "for edification and not for destruction" (2 Cor. 10:8; 13:10), for building others up, not for tearing them down.

Is that how you use your position and authority? Do you exercise leadership in order to accomplish the best interests of those who follow you? As they carry out your directives, are they built up in Christ, or torn down?

come again I will not spare— ³since you seek a proof of Christ speaking in me, who is not weak toward you, but mighty in you. ⁴For though He was crucified in weakness, yet He lives by the power of God. For we also are weak in Him, but we shall live with Him by the power of God toward you.

⁵Examine yourselves *as to* whether you are in the faith. Test yourselves. Do you not know yourselves, that Jesus Christ is in you?—unless indeed you are disqualified. ⁶But I trust that you will know that we are not disqualified.

⁷Now I[a] pray to God that you do no evil, not that we should appear approved, but that you should do what is honorable, though we may seem disqualified. ⁸For we can do nothing against the truth, but for the truth. ⁹For we are glad when we are weak and you are strong. And this also

💡 13:10

we pray, that you may be made complete. ¹⁰Therefore I write these things being absent, lest being present I should use sharpness, according to the authority which the Lord has given me for edification and not for destruction.

Final Words

¹¹Finally, brethren, farewell. Become complete. Be of good comfort, be of one mind, live in peace; and the God of love and peace will be with you.

¹²Greet one another with a holy kiss.

¹³All the saints greet you.

¹⁴The grace of the Lord Jesus Christ, and the love of God, and the communion of the Holy Spirit *be* with you all. Amen.

13:7 ªNU-Text reads *we*.

Paul's method of leadership reflected a unique style of authority that Jesus encouraged. See "Servant-Leaders," Matt. 20:25–28.

Notes

Notes

Notes

Notes